DARE TO SHARE!

Communicating
the Good News

DARE TO SHARE!

Communicating the Good News

MARNEY PATTERSON

ⲧ̄ⲧ̄ⲧ PUBLICATIONS
Invitation to Live Ministries
7718 Yonge Street
Thornhill, Ontario, Canada
L4J 1W2

1st Printing 1977
1st Reprint 1978
2nd Reprint 1980
3rd Reprint 1988

Unless otherwise indicated, Scripture quotations
are from the King James Version.

Published by **ITL PUBLICATIONS**
(a division of Invitation to Live Ministries)

Printed by: Publications Chrétiennes Inc.
230, rue Lupien
Cap-de-la-Madeleine, Québec, Canada
G8T 6W4

Printed in Canada

ACKNOWLEDGMENTS:

I would like to especially thank David Nadeau who read this book in manuscript. His journalistic wisdom and skill have been of enormous assistance to me.

I am also most grateful to the Reverend Bailey Snow and my secretary Beatrice Jackson who made many valuable suggestions.

Marney Patterson

"Take us, then, Lord and use us,
   to tell what we have heard,
   And all the minds of millions
   Shall feed upon your word."
               (From the hymn by Charles Jeffries, 1924)

CONTENTS

Introduction— Edward W. Scott, Primate,
           Anglican Church of Canada........15

PART I

Foreword..19
1. The Sense of Urgency...............................23
2. Doing More!..28
3. Holy Boldness..37
4. Expecting Miracles..................................41
5. The Starting Point of Christian Witness........47
6. The Content of Our Message.....................61
7 Personal Evangelism: A Way of Life..............75

PART II

8. Our Primary Task...................................84
9. Opportunities Abound!...........................91
10. Household Fellowships:
    Coffee Cup Evangelism...........................98
11. Mass Evangelism: Talking to Ourselves?.....110
12. The Spiritual Climate.............................118

Introduction

Mr. Patterson is dealing with an area to which the Anglican Church of Canada, as well as other branches of the Christian Church, needs to give particular attention.... The Proclamation of the Good News of Jesus Christ. He approaches this area of concern with both sensitivity and deep insights into the essential place which "love" and "respect" for individual persons must have in the process of evangelism if it is to be expressive of the true nature of the Word proclaimed.

Mr. Patterson writes of the need which challenges us to achieve a better balance between particular aspects of our total mission. He has shown me in this book that he recognizes and knows how to deal with one of our most basic problems...how to get individual Christians and groups of Christians to go beyond the incomplete action of just proclaiming the Word.

By nature of his own calling, Mr. Patterson focuses attention on the need for "proclamation"...a more vigorous, vital proclamation than we have been displaying in recent time. This is good. This book should stimulate others to produce companion books to emphasize the deep nature of worship as both giving expression to and calling for corporation action and responsibility in all areas of the world God created and sustains through His love.

Edward W. Scott,
Primate,
Anglican Church of Canada.

PART I

Foreword

WHAT IS EVANGELISM?

Evangelism is encounter. It is confronting people with the Person of Jesus Christ. While this may result in the acceptance or rejection of the Person and claims of Christ, evangelism cannot take place without confrontation.

James Stewart sees the starting point of such evangelism as "the realization that we have a faith to proclaim and a command to proclaim it. The faith which we are commanded to proclaim is that Christ died for the ungodly...coming into the world to save sinners and redeem us from the curse of the law." [1] "There is no evangelism," writes James I. Packer, "where this specific message is not declared." [2]

To evangelize is to be obedient to Christ's command to preach the Gospel to the whole world. The Church today must realize that in uttering these words, Christ was not merely expressing a hope or indulging in wishful thinking. Nor was He making a request. A King is not in the habit of doing either.

His is the royal prerogative, complete with the right to command and the power to enforce. Christ's divine imperative to evangelize the world is a task demanding the obedience and commitment of the entire Church—ministers and laity alike. The task, to be shared by all Christians and not just a selected or elected few, finds its inspiration in what Andrew did for his brother—saying, "We have found the Messiah," and bringing him to Jesus.

It is distressing and disturbing that the Christian community follows the world's pattern of hiding behind labels. "I'm an evangelical," we say. But such a statement has absolutely no meaning unless we live for the Evangel with Whom we have had a personal encounter. The validity of our encounter with Him, whether it took place suddenly or over a period of time, is surely to be seen **not** in our professing to be an evangelical, but as with Andrew's "validity," in a passionate desire to have others come to know him.

But the driving and motivating force behind evangelism must be **more** than obedience. Simple obedience is but an expression of the consent of our will. By itself it can be cold and devoid of love, compassion and concern for the souls of men. Obedience, necessary as it is, is just not adequate as a foundation for an evangelism ministry. Paul, writing to the Corinthians says it is "the **love** of Christ which constrains us"—moves us to act, to evangelize, to fulfill our ministry of reconciliation (II Corinthians 5:14-20).

When touched by this love of Christ, we soon discover within ourselves a new capacity for loving our fellowman, a love which finds expression in a compulsion to share the Christ we know.

Love and love alone—for God and man—provides validity to a ministry of evangelism and an authentic Christian life. It is this love which separates true evangelism and Christian witness from scalp hunting of which there is all too much and which is not only a poor substitute for the real thing but is surely repugnant to God. All of us must make certain that we draw a clear distinction between love and number counting. A failure to do so not only leads to unfruitful ministries but could place us in the unhappy position of being more used by the devil than by God.

There is absolutely no substitute for true, sincere love in the sharing of the Christian faith. Moreover, it has to be a love which is readily seen by those we seek to win. The look in the eye tells the tale. I will never forget the look in the eyes of those who came to me in my unconverted days. I felt ill at ease, not only because of their unloving approach, but because it was plain to see the hypocritical insincerity in their eyes. These encounters only drove me further away from the Christ I did not know. It was the small or absent measure of true love in their lives that hindered. They sought not so much to win me to Christ but to win for themselves another credit—another notch in their pocket testaments, proclaiming, much like a wartime fighter pilot, ''Got another one.''

In seeking to evangelize (or bring others into a personal encounter with Christ) let the motive always be **love**: love for Christ and those for whom He died. Our sincerity will never be doubted if it can be readily seen in our eyes. It will speak clearly of our love and will warm and melt the hardest of hearts. Evangelism is love in action.

(1) James S. Stewart, *A Faith To Proclaim* (Charles Scribner & Sons, 1953)
(2) James I. Packer, *Evangelism and the Sovereignty of God* (Madison, Wisconsin, Inter-Varsity Press, 1961) p. 39.

Chapter 1

The Sense of Urgency

Now is the hour! For someone, somewhere, today is the day that life ends. For that person there will be no tomorrow.

Since there is no way to know whose day this is—who will not survive the day—we must accept the fact that it could be the final day for any one of us. This should bring us to see or realize our ministry with a driving sense of urgency. This, in turn, should lead us to make the most of each day and to seize every opportunity to present Jesus Christ to those we meet and to whom we minister.

I remember a Jewish friend and neighbour of some years ago. Although she was Jewish, neither she nor her husband practiced their faith. "I'm a Jew but I'm an atheist," she used to say. It didn't take long to discover that she was an atheist in the fullest sense of the word. Aside from that, she was charming, intelligent and a person whose courage I have yet to see equalled.

We were eating dinner one day when I received a

telephone call from her.

"Mr. Patterson," she said, "I wonder if you would be able to visit me."

"Could we make it Wednesday afternoon?" I said.

"I would prefer right now."

I left my family to finish their meal. She met me at the door and asked me to join her in the living room. Without preliminaries she said, "I've just come from Princess Margaret Hospital (Toronto's cancer centre) and they told me I have only six months to live." The most experienced minister is always staggered by such pronouncements and I am no exception. My stomach constricted, my heart was sick and I found it difficult to remain composed.

"I need you, Mr. Patterson," she said. "I'll need your help for these will be difficult days for my husband and son." That was so much like her, thinking of her family and giving so little thought to herself. "I'll need you too," she continued. "I'd like your companionship in these months, but..." (and it was a strong but) "I don't want your God or your religion, I just want someone I can turn to."

"I'll be around Leah," I replied and with those words I began to experience the sense of urgency—six months at the most! Six months was all the Lord and I had to reach this lovely soul with His love. I knew that unless she had a personal encounter with Jesus Christ before death, she would never enter the Kingdom of God.

The days and weeks passed all too rapidly and in spite of my many visits in her home, I felt an increasing sense of frustration as I was getting absolutely nowhere. From the very outset I had resolved, in spite of her atheism, to pray during every visit. This didn't offend her. Her response was simple, and in some ways, humorous. "That's perfectly all right," she said. "If it does you any good, go right ahead and pray." I prayed during every visit and was also most earnest in my prayers for her in my daily devotions as well as in the services at church.

As the months passed Leah's flesh virtually disappeared before our eyes. With the arrival of the sixth month, we knew the original prognosis was proving to be very accurate—for Leah there would not be a seventh month.

When out-patient treatment became inadequate Leah left home and entered hospital. Moved by the urgency of the moment, I cast all caution aside and endeavored to share with her lovingly and boldly the love of Jesus Christ. Her response, as always, was immediate and terse.

"That's enough! If you insist on talking about your God I'll call the orderly and have you removed from this room!"

I had no choice but to refrain. The last thing I wanted was to destroy what had become a very close relationship. I still believed, in spite of the lateness of the hour, God would provide the time and the place for her to experience His love.

With time against me, I sought advice from a friend who is a Christian Jew. I told him how I had approached Leah and he was quick to point out my mistake.

"You presented the Christian faith to this woman. Can't you see she does not want or even need the Christian faith? She needs to meet the person of Jesus Christ!"

Leah had been associating Christ with all the trappings, doctrine and **dogma** of the Christian

Church. Her real need was to know God's love for her in Jesus Christ. And with a new sense of anticipation I immediately visited the hospital. But to my utter dismay she was still unreceptive and even more deeply committed in her atheistic resolve. Then it happened. Praise God! The Lord opened the door.

"I don't want your God, all I want is your love," she said.

"Leah, that's just the point," I said. "My love for you comes from God—He is love. He loves me. He loves you. I have experienced His love and I'm trying to share it with you."

Then I left without a further word.

I returned the next day and as I came in the door, she managed to raise her hand towards me. She beckoned me to her bedside and said simply, "Pray with me." I did. It was a short and simple prayer to ask God's blessing on her.

When I finished I said, "Leah, you are going to have to meet this man Christ and know His love for you."

"I did—last night."

The evidence of her personal encounter with Christ was written all over her face and reflected in the peace now so evident in her whole demeanor. And so it was through this beautiful woman that God not only proved His faithfulness, but showed the wonderful power of His love.

Leah died that night and I have absolutely no doubt as to Whose company she keeps as I record her story.

Stories similar to this can be related by any number of people. I tell Leah's story for one purpose only—to demonstrate that there must always be a sense of urgency which impels us to share the love of God in Christ now, today, at this hour, with this or that person. For who knows? Perhaps for that person there will be no tomorrow. Perhaps there will be no tomorrow for us either.

Chapter 2

Doing More!

In his book **Letters to Young Churches**, J.B. Phillips translates Romans 9:1-3 as follows:

> Before Christ and my own conscience in the Holy Spirit I assure you that I am speaking the plain truth when I say that there is something that makes me feel very depressed, like a pain that never leaves me. It is the condition of my brothers and fellow Israelites and I have actually reached the pitch of wishing myself cut off from Christ if it meant that they could be won for God.

Why was Paul so depressed by the plight of fellow Jews? Why did his heart ache for them? Did they not have a zeal for God? Were they not God's chosen people? "Yes," writes Paul in Romans 10, "they have a zeal for God but not according to knowledge, for they, being ignorant of God's righteousness, are going about to establish their own righteousness and have not submitted themselves unto God."

As a Christian Jew, Paul's heart ached for his Jewish brethren. He knew they were continuing to be just like he had been in the days before his conversion. He saw them doing just as he had done—continuing their zealous pursuit of God—a pursuit based on ignorance. Paul knew that if that ignorance continued, it would deprive them of the very salvation they so eagerly sought.

Paul also knew that even now, as they sincerely sought to please God "through their own righteousness," in their great state of ignorance they were blind to the fact that they were living apart from Him. Their sins were unforgiven, the peace of God was not in their lives. That which they sought more than anything else (the gift of Eternal Life) would never come to pass for them. Paul knew, as few others knew, that his people were damned as they lived. Little wonder he was so depressed when he thought of them. Is it any wonder that he stood willing to see himself "cut off from Christ if it meant that they could be won for God"? Paul's aching heart cried out continually for Israel "that they might be saved."

There is absolutely no doubt that Paul believed Jesus to be "the way, the truth and the life." He believed that He and He alone could bring a person into a relationship with God the Father.

One of the greatest needs of today's Church is for all members to acquire an aching heart like Paul's. As Christians we're aware of our Lord's command to be witnesses for Him. We will readily acknowledge the necessity of being obedient to His command, but somehow this obedience just doesn't seem to be applicable to us—it doesn't move us to witness, to share the faith or to seek the lost. Why?

Obedience for the sake of obedience is not adequate. Jesus never intended it to be. His compassionate heart ached for mankind, an aching which expressed itself ultimately on the Cross of Calvary where he was cut off from God (My God, why hast Thou forsaken Me?) in order that man might be reconciled to the Father.

"I too," said Paul, "have actually reached the place of wishing myself cut off from Christ if it meant that they (the Jews) could be won for God." Paul knew that his being cut off from Christ would not achieve anything for his Jewish brethren. He also knew, in the absence of such an experience, he must give his life (body, mind, spirit) in another way, in total service, "that they might be won for God." He was so depressed by the spiritual poverty of his brethren that his heart ached. We Christians of the twentieth century desperately need that same aching heart.

How does one acquire such a heart? By realizing the extent or the perimeters of God's condemnation. Within the truths of the Gospel it is plain that all men, women and children who have not had a personal encounter with Christ, all those who have not responded to His love and all those who have not received Him as personal Saviour—are condemned before God. "He that believeth not is condemned already, because he hath not believed in the name of the only begotten Son of God." This is not unkind judgment of one's fellowman. It is the acceptance of the truth as expressed by the living Son of God. When we accept our Lord's teachings on the state of the unbeliever as being literally true, then and only then will we, like Paul, be "depressed" and "have a pain that never leaves us." Then we will have the aching heart that will **move us** to pray for and to witness to the unbeliever. We will be moved to action only when we clearly understand the actual condition, the spiritual poverty and sickness and the utter hopelessness of man apart from God.

Some of today's newspapers publish pictures of children who are available for adoption. In many instances, they are youngsters the agency is having some difficulty in placing because of some physical defect, retardation or mixed racial background. This has proven a very successful method for encouraging adoption, largely because of the fact that many parents, or would-be parents, have been moved by the needs of the children they have seen and read about in the paper. The news editors know, and we as Christians must learn, that the heart moves people to action.

I have a minister friend who has five adopted children, all brothers and sisters. In spite of his very low salary he was prompted to offer these youngsters a loving home. It started when he opened his paper and read how they lost their parents in an auto accident. The hearts of this minister and his wife ached for these children in the time of their great need, moving them to share their love and their home.

This is what Paul talks about in his letter to the Christians in Rome. The recognition of human needs creates within us the aching heart. The aching heart moves us to action. Surely it was these two factors that compelled Paul to give himself unsparingly to a ministry of evangelism. In spite of ill health and the many hazards of travel, he covered Asia Minor, its villages, towns and cities, declaring passionately to Jew and Gentile ''the unsearchable riches of

Jesus Christ."

Do you realize that the extent of your concern for those of your own family is a good measurement of your commitment to Jesus Christ? I never cease to be amazed at the large number of Christians who openly admit they do not pray for the unbelieving members of their families. Is this because of an absence of love? All too often it is the absence of the aching heart, based on an unwillingness to accept that their dear ones are numbered among those who are condemned "because they have not believed in the only begotten Son of God."

When we come to truly and fully believe in the desperate state of man apart from God, and fully believe in the love of God for man in his desperate state, **then** our loved ones and their spiritual needs will become for us a primary concern. This concern will move us to pray in a spirit of love with a sense of urgency for their salvation.

The same belief will inevitably prompt us to do everything humanly possible to share with them the Good News of Jesus Christ. I have never been, nor am I now, happy with my own efforts to reach my loved ones and friends. But as I write these words, I write with the resolve to do even more in the years that lie ahead.

The truth of the old saying, "If you are going to lift someone up you must be on higher ground," is more applicable to the Christian life and ministry than any other walk or calling. It is my regret that not every professing Christian accepts this truth as being self-evident.

I have met many ministers and a large number of lay leaders at home and abroad who confess they have never made a serious attempt to secure themselves on the higher ground. Others who were on that higher ground have since lost it. They now find themselves losing the battle for the souls of men. It is an inevitable regression—to lose your own battle is to lose the battle of helping others in this world.

The higher ground is secured and held only when we, as His disciples, discipline ourselves to have, at any price, regular, serious and enriching daily devotions.

"He that abideth in me and I in him, the same bringeth forth much fruit: for without me you can do nothing."

Our abiding in Christ is rooted in our daily communing with Him and our fruitfulness depends on this taking place. For this in not **our** ministry but **His.** We are nothing more than His ambassadors. We represent Him and speak for Him. Can we do either if we are not in touch with Him?

Let us pursue this metaphor of "ambassador." In international affairs, the ambassador is an important person. While residing in a foreign country, he speaks to that country and its leaders on behalf of his home government. When he speaks it is his government and leader speaking through him. His presence in that foreign country is the presence of his actual government, so much so that the consulate and its grounds are actually considered part of his home country. Both he and his staff, and the actual building and grounds, are protected by diplomatic immunity—freedom from intrusion or prosecution.

What a changed world this would be if we as "ambassadors for Christ" could grasp the full import of what Paul is saying when he describes the true nature of Christian discipleship.

We are His ambassadors. We do represent Him, however inadequately that may be. We speak on His behalf—as though it is He who is speaking. The Church (His Body) is His consulate in the kingdom of this world.

How can we represent Him if we are not in touch with Him? How can we speak as He would have us speak, act as He would have us act, unless we are in constant consultation with Him? Obviously, we cannot! Why do so many of us insist on trying to exercise and continue His ministry without Him? Perhaps Christ Himself anticipated our drifting and stubbornness when He said, "without me you can do nothing."

We can talk about evangelism in its many forms and we can plan and initiate new methods and techniques, but it is a waste of time unless it begins where all evangelism begins—on our knees, humbling ourselves before Him whom we represent. We must seek His guidance, wisdom and power as we learn His will. And in the midst of this communing with Him, we will discover we have found for ourselves the higher ground, from which we, through Him, may lift others up to see Him as the way, the truth and the life.

The personal devotional life, which must be carefully disciplined, is as much an integral part of evangelism as the personal testimony, the preaching of the Word, or the altar call. Foolish is the person who prepares to share his personal faith in Christ crucified and who looks for the miracle of rebirth to take place through his sharing without first consulting with the One he seeks to share.

A meaningful devotional life takes different forms for different people and to find that which best meets one's own situation can manifest itself as quite a struggle. Very briefly, here is something of my own struggle to secure the higher ground. I feel in my heart I have attained this higher ground and as I look back it is not hard to remember how difficult it was to find this ground and how even more hard it is to keep it.

The greatest single threat to the Christian's devotional life is change—change in environment, change of routine, change within the family structure. When I travel, as I do very frequently in our Crusade ministry, this quite naturally changes the pattern of my life, including my devotions. It took too long to recognize this as a threat to my Christian life and ministry. I have found the same is true of vacations. Isn't it easy to let our spiritual life deteriorate as we travel the open road and leave the more structured, regulated and habitual life behind?

Another kind of change, though it brings even more joy than a summer vacation, can be an even greater threat. The arrival of the first child in a family can be one of the greatest threats to a married Christian's life, arising out of the transference of time, attention and affection. The baby's arrival is no less a threat to the devotional life of the parents, whether laity or clergy. The arrival of the child creates change—a radical change in living patterns which poses a threat to both personal and family devotions.

My wife and I found the search for a meaningful devotional life to be a real struggle. But it was a struggle which was infinitely worthwhile because it provided a secure foundation for our ministry, our marriage and a happy home. As the years passed, we found our pattern changing every few years through normal circumstances, be it a new child or otherwise. We have found what we think is the best routine for our present situation.

I normally rise at 6:30 a.m., wash, rouse my wife and go off for my devotions. My wife then washes up, wakes the children and while they are rising and preparing for school, has her devotional period. At breakfast we have a brief period (less than ten minutes) of family devotions. This, composed of Scripture reading, brief extemporaneous prayers shared by all, the Lord's prayer, concludes with grace. After breakfast, when the children have departed for school, my wife and I have a further time together in prayer. It's not ideal, but at the moment it seems to fit both our situation and our need. We will change the format if and when circumstances demand it—which they eventually will. Our devotions before retiring at night are very brief. My wife and I have found that for us, morning is the most practical time for a meaningful devotional period. Others may find the evening is more convenient. Each to his own way as the Lord leads. And He always will!

Chapter 3

Holy Boldness

One of the greatest needs in the life of today's Church is boldness—a holy boldness which is the direct result of the presence and power of the Holy Spirit in the lives of believers.

Writing to fellow Christians in Ephesus, Paul acknowledges his own need of such boldness, knowing that without it he could not be used as a mighty instrument of God's purpose. "Pray for me," he writes, "that utterance may be given unto me, that I may open my mouth boldly" (Ephesians 6:19-20). And for what purpose? "To make known the mystery of the gospel for which I am an ambassador in bonds." Such utterance and boldness was given to Paul. I say this because if anything leaps out of the pages of the Book of Acts it is that he and his companions pursued a ministry of boldness and fearlessness. Men everywhere were attracted to them and listened to their message, transfixed by their dynamic witness and transformed by the Holy Spirit (Acts 9:28,29 and 14:10).

Can't you see how desperately we need this boldness in our day? If there ever was a time when His ambassadors (that's us) needed a holy boldness, it is now! Never before in history has there been more need for men and women to stand up unafraid and say boldly, "Thus saith the Lord."

Wake up to the fact that ours is no ordinary message, nor is our ministry a simple, mundane task. As His ambassadors we are men of God, speaking as we are moved by the Holy Spirit. We must, as Paul says, "speak boldly as we ought to speak" (Ephesians 6:20).

Isn't it all too evident that we are not speaking as boldly as we ought to speak in the Church? Why?

There are two basic reasons. First, we as Christians are all too often self-motivating. We operate under our own steam. This was never intended. The power in every person's ministry must emanate from the Holy Spirit in his life. Without the Holy Spirit there is no power, and without the power there can be no life-giving force which alone results in the transformation of human lives.

That there is some boldness in the ministry is true—but at times it is a boldness which is of man and not of the Holy Spirit—making it offensive and repugnant to God.

Such man-created boldness dishonours everything that is holy in the ministry of evangelism and in the life of the Church. There is no place for such boldness, nor for such a man, in the ambassadorial ranks of the King of Kings.

The second reason for the absence of the holy boldness in the lives of believers today—both laity and ministers—is the fear of man. How frequently do we refrain from speaking as boldly as we ought to for the very simple reason that we fear the response from those to whom we are talking? This fear strangles the believer into a life of silence, the end result of which is a sense of frustration and futility with the whole of one's Christian life.

While this may seem a strange affliction for a Christian, it is not uncommon. Everyone is human and as humans we have latent fears and phobias which are quickly brought to the surface when we find ourselves doing something beyond the realm of normal activity—be it witnessing in public or having to speak boldly of and for Him. You are not alone. Indeed, you are numbered with the majority of Christians who, like myself, have had similar experiences.

In my early college years I was bound and chained by my fear of man. It was so bad that I was tied in emotional knots when doing something as simple as reading Scripture in a chapel service. And all of this was in spite of my four years in broadcasting during which I had spoken daily to thousands of people.

The problem was a simple one with a simple solution—I was relying on myself. Then a close and knowledgeable friend drew my attention to Paul's fatherly reminder to young Timothy: ''God hath not given us the spirit of fear, but of power, and of love and of a sound mind'' (II Timothy 1:7).

I cannot begin to count the number of times I have turned to this verse for encouragement throughout the past fifteen years. Time after time, in the midst of some very difficult situations, I have felt fear and anxiety pulling at my heart. Such fears are of my own creation. I have learned their roots are in my tendency to rely on my own wisdom and ingenuity, rather than on the presence, guidance and power of the Holy Spirit.

"If God be for us, who can be against us?" writes Paul. To which I silently add, "and if God be for us, where then is the need of fear?"

God did not give His ambassadors the spirit of fear, but rather power, love and a sound mind. Applied as they should be, these will lead inevitably to a holy, bold and fearless proclamation of the Gospel of Christ, the end results of which are never in doubt.

Chapter 4

Expecting Miracles

Some years ago it was my privilege to conduct a "quiet day" for a ministerial association in a large city. As my subject I chose a favorite theme—"A Sense of Expectancy." I said God's spokesmen must always enter the pulpit with a real sense of expectancy. They should expect and look forward to the miracle of rebirth to take place right then and there in the lives of those listening to the Good News of Jesus Christ.

I spent some time elaborating on this sense of expectancy in preaching. I did my utmost to make the point that God has promised (and He is a keeper of His promises) to bring forth fruit if we will sow the seed of His word and do so expectantly. This holy promise is found in Isaiah 55:10, 11:

> For as the rain and the snow come down
> from heaven, and return not thither but
> water the earth, making it bring forth
> and sprout, giving seed to the sower and
> bread to the eater, **so shall my word be**

that goes forth from my mouth; it shall
not return to me empty, but it **shall**
accomplish that which I purpose and
prosper in the thing for which I sent it.

At the conclusion of the quiet day, one of the
ministers drove me home. We parked in front of my
house and he started to comment on the quiet day.
Then, without warning, he began to weep. He
regained his composure after a few moments.

"Marney," he said, "one thing you said today hit
me. Remember when you were talking about
expecting the miracle of rebirth to take place when
we preach? I've been preaching for almost thirty
years and I guess I never expected anything to
happen. You know, I don't know of a single
conversion that has resulted from my preaching."

My heart went out to him for he was a wonderful,
godly man, undoubtedly doing his best to serve
Christ faithfully in his denomination. But this man is
not alone. Indeed, his number is legion. I have found
dozens of such men in every city and country where
we have served—men who are fully committed in
their hearts to a ministry of evangelism, but who, for
one reason or another, have lost this sense of
expectancy. Nowhere is this more evident than in
their preaching. To call this a tragedy would be an
understatement. The place to begin to deal with it is
in our theological colleges and seminaries. Let us
teach men **what** to preach, let us teach men **how** to
preach and let us teach them to do so **expectantly.**

There are many who say, "I'd be a rich man if I had
ten cents for every time I've heard: 'Surely you
don't expect someone to be born again every time
you preach the gospel!' " This is like the question
Charles Spurgeon put to one of his students who had

just returned to college after a summer's ministry. The student was despondent because things had not gone well for him—he couldn't report even one conversion as a result of his summer preaching.

"Well," Spurgeon said, "surely you didn't expect a conversion every time you preached."

"No," replied the young man, "not every time."

"That's exactly why you didn't have any," Spurgeon replied.

I praise God for teaching me a lesson on expectant preaching in the very early years of my ministry.

My first crusade was held in a very large Anglican church in Eastern Canada. In preparation for the evening service we met for prayer and discussion with the minister of the host church. I quite casually told him of my plan to issue an invitation or altar call at the conclusion of the evening message. He was visibly shocked.

"Marney," he said, "it can't be done."

It was my turn to be shaken.

"You must remember," he said, "this is the most prestigious church in the whole of Eastern Canada. Our parish role includes most of the doctors, lawyers, judges and professors in this city. Anyone who has any place in society or a prominent position in the city worships here. They won't buy an altar call! It's just not done in a church such as this."

What now? What was I to do or say under the circumstances? What would you do? Remember boldness?

The Lord said it for me by prompting the host minister to add as an afterthought—"But, I'm not going to bring you 1,200 miles and tell you what to do."

I returned to my hotel room and throughout the

afternoon I alternately prayed and paced around the room, trying to discern whether this whole idea of an invitation was mine or God's. Sometime in the late afternoon, I reached a sense of peace about the whole matter, knowing Whose idea it was and what I must do.

After I preached the Good News that evening, I called for a time of quiet prayer and the commitment of our lives to Him.

At the conclusion of two minutes of silent prayer (it seemed like two hours) I asked those who were accepting Christ as their personal Saviour to fill out the decision cards which had been distributed at the beginning of the service.

"Bring them forward," I said, "while we are singing the next hymn, place them on the offertory plate and kneel at the altar rail."

Without further hesitation (but with butterflies in my stomach) I announced the invitational hymn. The first person to come down the long aisle of that church wasn't walking, he was hurrying! I was to discover in the after-service counselling period that he was one of the leading surgeons in that city, holding one of the most desirable degrees in the medical world, an F.R.C.S. from Edinburgh, Scotland. At 48 years of age he was soundly converted and miraculously transformed.

Seven others followed this man down the aisle that evening. For them it was the beginning of a new life in Christ. For me it was the beginning of a ministry of expectancy.

In addition to our sense of expectancy there is the message on which the expectancy is based. I can't emphasize enough that the content of our message has to be the Gospel. It is insufficient if it is anything less. This may seem very elementary, but on closer examination one soon discovers it is not as rudimentary as it first appears. This is how I learned my lesson on this point....

A friend and I, working as a team, were conducting a parish mission in Western Canada. I had preached the evening message and with a real sense of expectancy had issued an invitation to those committing themselves to Christ to come forward. No one responded. I was surprised and very disappointed. This was a new experience for me. There had always been response on previous occasions. What was the problem? I couldn't see it.

Following the service my disappointment and concern must have been quite evident.

"Marney, examine your message," my friend suggested.

"My message? What's wrong with my message?"

"Take it out and let's take a look at it," he said.

As I placed it on the table he said: "Now, show me where the Gospel is."

I was offended. He was suggesting I had not preached the Gospel. But search as I did, I could not find it on any page. It just wasn't there. I had expected God to transform lives when I had failed to lift up His Son, Jesus Christ. He who had promised "and I, if I be lifted up, will draw all men unto Me" had not been lifted up. The result was that no one had been drawn to Him. The failure was clearly mine.

Some years later I was part of a discussion meeting. There were 140 people present, seven or eight of whom were ministers. We were talking about witnessing and I took the role of an unbeliever. I suggested they "share" their Christian faith with me in order that I might be won for Christ. For almost an hour they talked about the Christian faith but not once did they give me the Gospel, the Good News of my redemption through Jesus Christ. They talked about faith. They talked around it. But not once did they share it with me. They committed the same error that I had committed many years before. The Gospel on both occasions was conspicuous by its absence.

The point here is that it is not enough for us to preach expectantly. God, the Holy Spirit, must always have the vehicle in and through which He can convict men of their sin, bring them to repentance and transform them by His power. That vehicle is the Gospel—the Good News of man's redemption in the shed blood of Jesus Christ. When this Good News is absent, our sense of expectancy is without foundation. We issue our call to commitment in vain. "Woe is me," Paul said, "if I preach not the Gospel." Indeed, woe to us all!

Chapter 5

The Starting Point of Witness

The starting point for us is to define what we are talking about when we talk about witnessing. We make a mistake, I think, all too frequently, in the Christian life of using terms without really clearly defining what we mean by those terms. This seems to me to be the most logical place to begin. And the best definition of witnessing is to be found in John's first epistle, the first chapter, third verse. John writes, "That which we have seen and heard declare we unto you, that you may have fellowship with us and truly our fellowship is with the Father and with His Son, Jesus Christ." A beautiful and accurate definition of witnessing. "That which we have seen and heard declare we unto you."

What John is doing here is pointing out a definition of witnessing which has not only religious implications, but is also a good definition of witnessing in any sense of the word.

For example, in our democratic system our courts of law have certain legal procedures which we follow. First of all, in a court of law that which makes it work is this whole process of having witnesses. Let me illustrate it this way. You are standing out on a street corner and you are present at a given time when an accident occurs, and as one who has been there when the accident occurred you may be called upon by the police to give testimony to what took place. You can give that testimony because you were there, and being there you **saw** it happen, and you also **heard** it happen. So when you are called into the trial and placed on the witness stand you will be asked to testify to that which you saw and that which you heard. And if, in your testimony, you start to tell the court what someone else told you, you will be stopped and you will be corrected. The defence attorney or the prosecution, as the case may be, will say, ''Now we don't want to hear what someone else told you, because that's hearsay evidence. What we want to hear is what **you** saw and what **you** heard. You are the witness. You were there. And that's what really matters.''

This is really the nub of the matter when it comes to Christian witness. If you are telling someone about what Jesus Christ has done for someone that you know about or with whom you are acquainted, God can use that. But that which He uses best is your **own** witness. Tell them what God has done for **you**: not what happened to a relative of yours, but what God has done for you that He might do for them.

That's the kind of witness which really counts. And I believe that's what John is coming to here in this first chapter of his in the third verse: ''That which **we** have seen and heard declare we unto you.'' That which the Christian, the committed Christian, has seen and heard is that, in the Biblical sense, he has "seen the light."

That is to say, he has come to see in his own mind and heart that Jesus Christ was and is God's Son, and as God's Son He did something for him. He died for him. He was the means and is the means of his salvation. And that's what Jesus Christ is for every Christian. He is the One who died in my place, bringing about my redemption, removing the alienation between myself and God and bringing about a reconciliation between God and myself.

When you have seen the truth of the Christian faith, this is what you have seen. And you have come to see it because you've heard it. Someone has articulated it, someone has expressed it from the pulpit or in a personal testimony. In some way you have come to hear the words of the Good News of Jesus Christ and in hearing them you have seen the truthfulness of what was being expressed and responded to it.

"That which we have seen and heard declare we unto you." Once we have seen it—the truth—once we have heard it and responded to it, then it is up to you, and to me, to share it.

The Christian faith properly understood and properly experienced cannot be kept to yourself. Not if you've really experienced it. If you have encountered Jesus Christ in your life, there is absolutely no way that you are going to be content or happy with keeping that experience to yourself. You want to share it. You feel a compulsion, a drive, to share it for an express purpose—that others might come to believe.

John says, "That which we have seen and heard declare we unto you." Why? "That you may have fellowship with us." And what is that fellowship?

"Truly our fellowship is with the Father (God the Father) and with His Son, Jesus Christ."

Having come into a fellowship with God, through His Son, Jesus Christ, and this meaning so much to you, you want all the world to have the same experience. And the best way for that to happen in and through you and me, is for us to share it. We share it with the hope and prayer that God will bless it to the hearts and minds of others that they too might come to see the truthfulness of what we are saying, and respond to it.

This brings us then to the WHY of witnessing. There are those who feel that Christian witness is an optional thing. We hear them say, "She can do it; I can't. She is a person who is quite articulate and finds it easy to express herself. I don't. And therefore obviously God has given to her the gift of witnessing. He hasn't given it to me. He is not looking for me to do it. He is looking for her to do it." This is a long way from the Scriptural truth.

God expects **all** of us to use our gifts, whatever they may be and however limited they may be, to witness to Him.

And so it is not an optional thing for you, for me, or for anyone else. It is not something you can opt out on and leave to someone else. We find in Scripture that God has actually **ordered** us to share the faith. And you see, because He is God and we are not, He has that prerogative. He can order us to do things and He **has** ordered us to witness to Him. Prior to His ascension into heaven, Jesus said to His disciples assembled in the city of Jerusalem, "Ye shall be witnesses unto Me in Jerusalem, in Judaea, and in Samaria and unto the uttermost part of the earth" (Acts 1:8).

Please note that He did not say, "Well, I'm leaving, I hope—I really hope—you fellows will get out and share what I've told you about Me." He didn't express a hope. Nor did He say, "I wish you would go out now and share this." He wasn't expressing a wish. He was **giving a command.** "You **shall** be witnesses unto Me." And inasmuch as He said that to all of His followers who were present on that occasion, He says the same thing to us. It's an order for every believer and it applies to us all.

In Mark's gospel, the 16th chapter and the 15th verse, we have it put in another way. "Go into all the world and preach (communicate) the gospel to every creature." And that's why the Christian Church sends people to the four corners of the earth. The Christian faith is unique in this respect.

There are all kinds of religions in the world today that feel no compulsion to go out into the rest of the world and share the faith. There is a reason for that. They don't believe it is necessary, because they've never been told to do it. They are under no obligation to do it. It is not so with the Christian.

From time to time there are those who will say, "What right do you have to go to India and force your faith on the Hindu and the Muslim?" There is only one answer to that. I haven't been told to force my faith on anyone, but I have been told to share God's love with **everyone.**

"Well, who told you?"

God told me. That's the justification for the Christian faith being carried to the four corners of the world.

Paul comes at this question of witnessing from a different direction, which is a very interesting one, fascinating and very powerful, when in the tenth chapter of Romans, the 9th and 10th verses, he writes:

> If thou shalt confess with thy mouth the Lord Jesus, and shalt believe in thine heart that God hath raised him from the dead, thou shalt be saved.
> For with the heart man believeth unto righteousness and with the mouth confession is made unto salvation.

Thus the true test as to whether or not you are a **true** believer is actually to be seen in whether or not you witness to Jesus Christ. It is Paul's expressed conviction, and a valid one it is, that if you believe Him in your heart then you will confess Him with your mouth. A lot of people have never really come to grips with this passage. I think if they had, they would have long since reassessed the nature and the extent of their commitment.

It is a very simple thing actually. What he is really saying is, "If you really believe anything in your heart, sooner or later you are going to talk about it." And when you stop and examine life, you find that this is true.

Parents are prone to talking about their children—we have four of them—and it's a natural thing. You're proud of your children. They are your flesh and blood. It's the most natural thing in the world to talk about your children. You get some people started on this subject and they'll never quit. It's the same thing with grandparents talking about their grandchildren. I have a cousin who just became a grandmother, and I was in a home recently where she was present. My wife said to her, "You've recently become a grandmother." Well, you couldn't get her to stop talking. She had the most beautiful granddaughter in the world. Nothing could compare with that child.

That's what Paul is talking about. That when you have love in your heart for someone, be it a child, a grandchild, a husband, wife or whoever it may be, it is natural to talk about that person who means so much to you.

Paul says that if you have really encountered Jesus Christ in your life and experienced His love, that's the way it is. You will have that same compulsion to share this Jesus Christ, His love and all that it means, with others.

So Christian witnessing is **not** an optional thing. We are under **orders** to share Christ and as true believers we are **compelled** by the way we feel about Him to share Him with others.

This has nothing to do with ability. God readily understands that some people can express themselves much more adequately than others. But it has nothing to do with that. He expects us all to witness. He knows some people will be better at it than others, for after all He did create us and give to each one of us a variety of gifts. Hence some people are better at playing the piano than others. I can play with one hand, my children can play with two.

God expects you, whoever you are, wherever you are, whatever the nature of your personality, however easily you express yourself, however difficult you find it, He still expects you to share your love of Jesus Christ. Because, you see, some people will respond (and God knows this) to those who find it difficult to express their faith because they more readily relate to them, having as they do the same difficulty in speaking to other people.

In 1969 I was ministering on the northern island of Hokkaido in Japan. My son, Stephen, who was fourteen at the time, was with me. To our utter amazement, the Chairman of the Crusade said to him, "Stephen, we would like you to give your testimony at the high school tomorrow."

Stephen said, "All right." That night when we were sitting in the hotel room he said, "Dad, they asked me to give my testimony."

I said, "Yes, I heard that. You were just behind me and I heard the conversation."

He said, "What'll I say?"

It's a good question, isn't it? "What'll I say?"

He had never given his testimony and here he was now going to face a high school audience of about 300 Japanese teenagers, guys and girls, and was going to have to do it through an interpreter. That led to quite an interesting conversation.

The next day he stood up before that audience. He was then, and still is when he is out of his element, shy. And he was **very** shy at that time. He stood there looking down at the notes he held in his hand. (You can readily put yourself in the position of a fourteen-year-old boy in that situation.) I don't know what I would have done. My heart went out to him. He had consented to do this and he was going to do it.

Well, he did. He never raised his head. He just shared with them his experience of Christ. It took about five minutes. I recorded it and my wife and I treasure it to this day.

The response was fascinating. They had appointed a young Japanese student, a girl, to express the gratitude of the group. She said, in her broken English, "Stevie, we love you. You're shy and so are we." The Japanese people are traditionally shy and so you see it took one with that kind of personality to really come across.

This is the way it is. You may be a shy person. You may not be given to expressing yourself readily. Recognize that God has given you a personality and that He wants you to use it. Give Him a chance and He will use you, probably with people who are much like yourself...who can best be reached through **your** personality.

There are any number of reasons why people do not witness. We've mentioned some of them already. In his second letter, Peter deals with another. In the third chapter, the 18th verse, he writes, "Grow in grace and in the knowledge of our Lord and Saviour Jesus Christ."

Some people are not sharing Jesus Christ because they are still spiritually retarded children. They are members of God's family, they've given their lives to Christ, they have encountered Him in their lives, of that there is no doubt. But they are still not sharing Him. Why? They haven't the confidence. Why? Because they have not reached that spiritual maturity which is necessary in order to share the faith. You have to **grow** in it. You have to grow in your understanding of it. It is only then that you can express it.

What is the Christian faith? We'll be talking about that in the next chapter under the title "The Content of Our Message." We must understand that message. We must grow in our knowledge and love of God. And we will never cease to grow, we should understand that. But God can use us and will use us to the extent that we grow. And so in the beginning of our Christian lives He may use us in some lives, and undoubtedly He will. But as we mature, as we become spiritual adults, we will find Him using us more and more, because we have come to a greater understanding and maturity in the Christian faith.

There is only one way I know that you can grow, and that is to feed yourself. As that is true physically, it is true spiritually. And therein is the problem. All too many committed Christians, those who have encountered Christ, have not grown and therefore have not been used to any large extent. Much of this is attributable to the fact that they are not feeding themselves.

Physically, if we are going to be healthy, we have such a nature that we must feed ourselves with regularity, preferably three times a day. Some of us might do it more—with some risk. But the normal procedure is three times a day. A child has to have those three meals, and if a child doesn't, then that child is going to have problems, physical, organic problems. It is not going to grow. We have all kinds of reminders of that when we see pictures on television and in the newspapers of children who don't have the food (in some of the Third World countries), who can't grow even though their parents would like them to grow. The wherewithal for their growth is not there, they can't be fed.

Well, as that is true physically, it is true spiritually. The extent to which we grow into spiritual adulthood is contingent on our feeding ourselves. Peter says, "Desire the milk of the word, the word of God that you may grow thereby" (I Peter 2:2).

It's possible perhaps for you to grow spiritually without reading the Word of God, but that spiritual growth will be extremely limited. What is necessary is a regular daily diet of feeding on the Word of God.

Not once a week, not once a month, but day by day, week by week, month by month, year by year. It is in the Word of God that we will find the nourishment for our spiritual growth.

This brings us to another very important point which I call the compelling force behind our Christian witness. The compelling force...perhaps the greatest force there is in Christian witness and that which God uses most...is love. In II Corinthians 5:14 we read, "For the love of Christ constraineth us (compels us)." That's what it is all about. Once we have reached spiritual maturity, we will find that nothing holds us back. Not because we find it is a good idea, not so much because God has told us, but our love for God and our love for Jesus Christ and our love for our fellowman, all drive us to share what God has done for us in and through Jesus Christ.

Paul puts his finger on it in these words, "For me to live is Christ" (Philippians 1:21). That's what we are talking about. The reason for your existence, the reason for your getting up in the morning and going out and living each day, is Christ. You live for Christ. Eating, sleeping, living and breathing Jesus Christ. And when that happens in your life, when that is the reason for your existence, you won't be long in discovering that God is using you with startling frequency in the lives of other people, in the lives of your family, your neighbours, your fellow workers, people in the church, people outside the church, in your social life. God is using you so much that it staggers you. One of the basic reasons for that is that you have given your all to living out your days for the primary purpose of living the most exciting life there is, because you are living day by day in the area of the miracle.

You know, there is a sense in which Christian witness is thought of as our going out hunting for people who just possibly may be interested in knowing something about the Christian faith. Well, that's true, but it is only true to a very small extent. In fact, I think for the most part it is exactly the opposite. It's not a question of our going out and hunting for people with whom we can share the Gospel, but rather we find God bringing us to them and them to us. That's what I find and I think that there are a great many people who have discovered that this is so.

We are in an itinerant ministry of evangelism and so people are inclined to think, "The Invitation to Live team is leaving Toronto and it's coming here to this community to evangelize, and we've invited them to do so." All that is true. But one of the things that has come home to us with great force in our team is that it is only partially true. We find that evangelism is not so much a question of going to a place to evanglize, but rather living the life; because that's what it is. It's a way of life. And when you live that life, it is not a question of moving from point "A" to point "B" to evanglize or to witness. It is a question of witnessing as you move from "A" to "B," and also after you arrive in "B" and then as you go home from "B" to "A."

We have had some thrilling, exciting experiences on any number of flights. In an aircraft you sit down—and no matter how large the plane, they still have the seats very close together so that they can get a maximum number of people on board—you're strapped in a safety belt and you are literally rubbing elbows with the people seated beside you. You can't possibly avoid it. So like it or not you are forced to encounter people and sooner or later you are going to find yourself talking to them. It's fascinating, in that kind of situation, how a conversation of a spiritual nature can develop—and you may not even start it.

I was flying down to the southern States some time ago and unfortunately I had not really had time to prepare myself adequately for the addresses I was to give. I was due to arrive in a couple of hours and I was working my head off on the plane, making some notes. The man in the seat beside me just couldn't contain himself. After a while, I could see he was sort of looking over my shoulder. (And you can't avoid that either.) We hadn't even introduced ourselves and he said to me, "Man, I've seen some writing, but I've never seen writing as bad as that in all my life." A total stranger! Well, I knew what he meant because I could hardly understand it myself. I was writing so fast and it was just scribble. But I had to get it on the paper as the thoughts were coming to me. And that opened up a discussion. He said, "What are you writing?"

"I'm writing an address I have to give at a Conference in Atlanta."

"What sort of an address?"

"Well, I'm in the fire and life insurance business (that's what the ministry is all about) and I'm giving an address on a particular phase of it." We got into quite an interesting conversation during which I disclosed that I was a minister. You see how that opportunity so readily opened up!

I could tell you story after story of this nature. Things that happened in a hotel dining room, things is a way of life in which you are living for Christ wherever you go, recognizing that God is more apt to bring the people in touch with you, rather than your going out looking for them. The main thing is to be prepared to talk about your faith when the opportunity arises.

Chapter 6

The Content of Our Message

The act of Christian Witness involves the sharing of a message. "That which we have seen and heard declare we unto you." There is that which we must declare. A message to be conveyed. And we find in the New Testament that this message is essentially the same no matter who is saying it.

If you take and examine the witness of Paul, Peter and their companions Silas, Barnabas and the like, you will find that in and through their ministries they came bringing the same message. It might have been said in different ways because their personalities of course were different. But the ingredients were the same. And it is absolutely essential for us, as it was for them, to know what the message is.

First, there is the BAD NEWS. The Christian message is called the Good News and rightly so because that's what it is. But you cannot understand the good news without knowing the bad news. The good news has no meaning at all, for anyone, unless he knows there is bad news too. Because the good news **becomes** good news when he understands the bad news.

The bad news, for the lack of a better term, is called SIN. In Romans 3:10 we read, "there is none righteous, no not one."

In Romans 3:23 we read, "For all have sinned and come short of the glory of God." Who has sinned? "...all have sinned." Who does that include? It includes the Indian in India, the Chinaman in China, the American in America, the Canadian in Canada...and that includes you and me.

Now in sharing your faith, the prerogative is not yours to tell anyone that he or she is a sinner. That is **not** your prerogative and it is not necessary. And you'll never get away with it. The moment you tell anyone that he or she is a sinner, you have lost your relationship with that person. The lines of communication are shattered. You have, in that person's mind, become a self-righteous individual and there is no way that you can change that. But it **is** necessary for people to see themselves as sinners. The best way I know to bring that about is to let God do it. In Christian witnessing, God does most of it. We are just instruments of His purpose. He does that which needs to be done, and if He doesn't do it, nothing is going to happen.

The easiest way I know of bringing people under a conviction of their situation before God is to take them to God's Holy Word and let them read it. What could possibly be easier than that? Take them to Romans 3:23. What does it say?

"For all have sinned and come short of the glory of God."Ask them..."Who does that include?"

"Well, it includes my mother-in-law, my brother,

my neighbour. and so on.''

"Who else does it include?''

"It includes everyone.''

"But who does 'everyone' include?'' Press it home.
Do it lovingly. kindly. diplomatically. But do it. for
there is an answer you need here and there is
absolutely no point in going any further until that
answer is forthcoming.

"Do you think that includes me?''

He may be reluctant to say "Yes'' but he must say
"Yes.''

"Where do you fit into this? Does it include you?''

"Yes!'' And until you have that "yes.'' there is no
point in going on.

He **must** see the bad news as applying to **him.** Now
you will find this comes with surprising ease.
Because the kind of thing I find is this: it's rather
startling how quickly people will put themselves in
that position if we give them a chance. They know
that they've done wrong. and are doing wrong. It's
a rare person indeed who doesn't.

You might have an atheist sitting in front of you and
in spite of the fact that he doesn't believe in God.
it's interesting how readily he'll admit he does
wrong. even if it's just against some power external
to himself.

People will admit their sinfulness. They may not
call it sin. but the important thing is that they admit
the fact of wrong. The Bible calls it sin. That's where
it begins...because the **good news** is how God dealt
with that sin. So you see, it is necessary to have (A)
before (B). (B) is only understood in the light of (A).

Second, we have the LAW. There are so many
people who are sincerely endeavoring to live
according to God's law, and they feel that if they

keep that law, with some measure of success, that they will be in the family of God; God will forgive them of their sins, take them into His family and give them eternal life. Nothing could be further from the truth. Because, you see, the law was not given for that purpose at all. And this is where there is a tremendous amount of confusion in the lives of church-going people today who are trying to keep the law.

The law was given for the purpose of making people aware of their sins. That is its intended purpose. "For by the law is the knowledge of sin" (Romans 3:20). You can't break a law unless there is a law. That's what Paul is pointing out. "For by the law there is the knowledge of sin."

It doesn't bring you into a relationship with God. It makes you well acquainted with the fact that you don't have that relationship. That's what the law does.

Then, in Galatians 2:16, Paul says, "Man is not justified (he's not made right with God) by the works of the law, but by faith in Jesus Christ. For by the works of the law shall no flesh be justified in His sight."

You cannot be made right, or just, or sinless before God by performing the works of the law. God never intended that to be so; and yet so many people are sincerely trying to approach Him that way.

Third, there is GRACE. What does the word mean? It means unmerited favour. God giving to you and to me that which we do not deserve. That's grace.

In Ephesians 2:8,9 we read: "By **grace** are you saved through faith; and that not of yourselves: it is the gift of God: Not of works, lest any man should boast." "By grace (God giving to you that which you do not deserve) you are saved." Saved from what? Saved from the results of your sins which you have admitted.

"By grace are you saved through **faith.**" The exercising of your faith which brings you to commitment. In **faith** you accept Jesus Christ for what He was and is, the Son of God, your Saviour because He died to save you from the results of your sins, to remove that which stands in the way between you and God, and to bring about a reconciliation with Him.

And none of this is because we deserve it. There isn't anything you or I could possibly do to merit or deserve the love of God. Not if we really know what we are like.

What is there that we could possibly do that would make us deserving of God's love and make us deserving of the fact that He would send His Son to die in our place? Now how in the world could we possibly deserve that? We can't! But God gives it to us anyway. Not because of what we are but **in spite of what we are.** That is the measure of God's love.

You see, this is where God's love is so different from human love. For the most part, human love is experienced because the love is merited. You love a person in most instances because of what he or she is. Human love is based on how we feel about people, and because of what they are. It is not so with God's love. Because, you see, we're not loveable. We are undeserving of God's love. But that is the beauty of His love. He loves us in spite of ourselves. And in spite of ourselves He gave His Son to show us that love. That's grace. God giving to us that which we do not deserve.

That brings us to the fourth point: the LOVE of

which I have been speaking. "God so loved the world that he gave His only begotten Son that whosoever believeth in Him should not perish but have everlasting life" (John 3:16).

Now, it is possible for a person to be well acquainted with the fact that God loves the whole world but, for any number of reasons, to not really come to grips with the fact he is a part of that world which God loves. This was my problem. I had known that God loved the whole world. I had learned that in my Sunday School days. That's what the faith is all about...God's love. But to know His love is for the whole world is one thing, and to experience that love in your own heart and life is something quite different. You experience that love when in your mind you understand that it's for **you**, individually, and when in your heart you respond to it. For it is in the heart, the seat of human affection, where we experience the love of both man and God.

Some years ago in Halifax, Nova Scotia I sat at the dining room table in a hotel with Dr. Franz Uhler, who now resides in the Ottawa Valley. He was, at the end of the last War, the President of Czechoslovakia. He responded to God's love when the communists buried him in a hole in the ground—like a rat—in the courtyard of a prison. Here he was stripped of his political position and prestige. Here he literally lost the clothes on his back. Through six months he lived in a hole in the ground which wasn't large enough for him to stand up; where he saw neither the light of day nor the face of man but was fed through a straw. He lost everything. There in the darkness and dampness and the loneliness of that hole, he experienced the love of God because he responded to a message which he had heard so many years before.

He said: "There was nowhere else I could turn."

I can remember talking to a probation officer years ago in a Crusade. When I arrived in this town, the United Church pastor came to me and said: "I would like you to talk to a man here in our community. He is searching for the Christian faith: I don't know what his problem is. I've talked to him. Every pastor in this town has talked to him at one time or another, but there is something that he can't come to grips with, and we don't know what it is."

I answered, "I don't know what it is, and I don't know what I can possibly say that hasn't been said already."

He said, "Give it a try." So I told him I would. The next afternoon I found myself seated in the pastor's study talking to this probation officer. He was a married man with three children. He said, "Where do we start?"

I responded, "I haven't the slightest idea. I don't know you; I've never met you before. So there's only one way open to us. We start at the beginning, Al." I opened my Bible and handed it to him and said, "Read that passage—John 3:16—to me."

"I don't need to read that to you. I memorized that in Sunday School days." And he started to say it.

I said, "Never mind saying it. Read it to me." So he started to read it to himself. I said, "Read it out loud, Al." And he did.

He put the Bible back down on the desk and said, "So what!"

And then I was led to say something I had never said to anyone before. (God the Holy Spirit always leads if we give Him enough time.) "Al, you get that world out of there and get yourself in."

"God so loved me (Al) that He gave His only begotten Son that if I (Al) believed in Him, I should not perish but have everlasting life. Read it and put your name in."

He looked at me, picked up the Bible and read it. "God so loved me...Al..." and there was dead silence. It seemed like hours, but it was only a minute or two, and then he put the Bible down and said, "Isn't that stupid? All these years I've never seen that God's love was for me. I always applied it to the world and never saw that it was for **me** that Jesus died, as part of the world." Moments later he committed his life to Jesus Christ.

That man is not alone. Most people know that Jesus Christ died for the whole world. If you ask them, they will tell you that. All of you know that. But there are a lot of those people who do not see themselves as **part** of the world for which Jesus Christ died. Do you?

Which brings us to our **response**, which is faith. Point five—We find the experience of God's love through FAITH. There is no other way. In Hebrews 11:6 we read: "Without faith it is impossible to please Him: for he that cometh to God must believe that He is and that He is a rewarder of them that diligently seek Him." Now there, right there in those last words, we find a problem which is common to a lot of people. "He is a rewarder of them that diligently seek Him." The onus, the responsibility, is on us to seek Him. And to me that makes a lot of sense. Because, you see, that's the way He knows we want Him. When we seek this personal relationship and experience of His love, when we seek it, we will find it.

"Ye shall seek me and find me when you search for

me with all your heart" (Jeremiah 29:13). And you don't find Him until you seek Him and search for Him. The moment you do, it matters not where you are or who you are, you will find Him. When you're open to Him in your heart, you will, in that moment, find Him and be found by Him.

There is an inclination on our part to write off what has happened before our commitment. We shouldn't do this. Paul met Jesus Christ on the road to Damascus, but surely that's not where his spiritual journey began. He had had a very close relationship with God. He had been, for many a year, a deep, sincere, religious person.

I cannot possibly separate the giving of my life to Jesus Christ—my commitment to Him in the quietness of my college room—from the fact that I had been a lay preacher and a Sunday School teacher, and that I was confirmed at twelve years of age, and baptized at about six weeks. You see, all of that was part of my spiritual journey which came to a head at that moment in my college room. God had been very much at work in my life through those years.

Though you make a "point-in-time" commitment of your life to Jesus Christ and experience His love at that time, there have been many meaningful things that have taken place in your life through the years which have led you to that time. I believe this to be true of most people. Even people who have never been in the church...God has been speaking to them out there, outside of the church, in any number of ways, But it comes to a head through the exercising of their faith, when to Him and to themselves they admit that they want to experience His love in their hearts and the new life He offers.

And that can happen without our saying a word.

Now in leading someone along the way in this search and ultimately into this encounter with Christ, it is helpful for you to help them make that commitment. Many people need that help. Not all people. When I was used of God in the situation with the probation officer and he said, "Isn't it stupid, I've never seen this..." the next thing he said was "Let us pray." And he prayed. And that is where he made his commitment to Christ. I didn't need to say any more.

There are those occasions of course when you talk to people and they admit their need. They recognize that they now understand what this is all about; that this is the kind of life they want. I am very fond of using a question at that time, which is this: "Is there anything in your life which prevents you from making that commitment to Jesus Christ now?" In most cases there isn't.

"Would you do it now?"

How do they do it? I call it the A, B, C's of the Christian faith.

> (A) Have them **ADMIT** their condition and their need. Admit their sin, express their sorrow for it and their need of forgiveness of the same.
> (B) Have them express their **BELIEF** that Jesus Christ died for them personally to "reconcile them unto God," and
> (C) based on that, have them **COMMIT** their lives totally to Him.

Having explained the A, B, C's, suggest having a prayer together based on these steps.

"I would like to have a prayer with you, with your consent, in which I pray, phrase by phrase, and you repeat it after me. What we are going to do is this:

"(A) We are going to admit your need of the experience of God's love and forgiveness. You've already told me you understand that and it doesn't give you any problems.

"(B) In this prayer we are going to say this sentence (without putting words in your mouth because you've already said this to me) that you believe that Jesus Christ died for you, and then

"(C) give your life to Him.

"Would you say that prayer with me?"

I don't think I have ever been turned down when I have made this suggestion.

And so you say the prayer. "I acknowledge my sin." And that's it. That's the admission. "I stand in need of your forgiveness and reconciliation. I believe that Jesus Christ died for me personally to remove my sins and I now, in gratitude and love, give my life to Him" That's it. And God will bless that.

Now a person can say that prayer with you or in some cases may not want to. Some may want to go home and do it on their own. Bear in mind that in Christian witnessing you are not out on a spiritual scalp hunting expedition where you are trying to cut a notch in your New Testament—you got another one! That is not what it is all about.

You are God's instrument and when this person makes a commitment it must be because God is bringing it about, not you. And there's a world of difference which can be so readily seen. If you bring it about by pressure or coercion, then you ought to know that in all probability nothing will happen. Because God isn't in it. But if the willingness is there, on the part of the person, to make that commitment, then lead him through it. Ask him to express his conviction that this is what he wants.

Some time ago in the midst of a crusade in Smiths' Falls, Ontario our music director, Bill McCaul, walked into the hotel dining room to have a cup of coffee. He was the only person in the room. Right out of the blue one of the waitresses, who was having coffee with another waitress at the other side of the room, called out to him, "How can I be sure I'm saved?" Bill was staggered. You don't expect that when you walk into a hotel dining room for a cup of coffee!

He said, "Bring your coffee over here and let's talk about it." And so they talked. He explained the Christian faith to her. But he didn't feel led to bring her to a commitment. He felt this was not the time. A Roman Catholic woman, she was sincere in asking a very good question which was important to her. "How can you be **sure** that you are saved from your sins?" That's what she was really asking.

Bill came up to my hotel room, quite excited about all of this, and related the story to me. So we prayed for her and we continued to pray for her over the next day or two.

A few days later I went down for a coffee break and it so happened the same waitress was on duty along with another one. When she came over to bring my coffee, I said to her quite casually, "I understand you had quite an interesting conversation with my colleague."

She said, "Yes, I did. I found it very helpful."

"Well," I said, "sit down if you've got a moment." She sat down, and I said to her, "He tells me he shared with you the Christian faith."

"Yes," she replied, "he did."

I asked, "Did you understand it?"

"Yes, he explained it very clearly," she responded.

I asked, "What is there that stands in the way of your making a commitment, giving your life to Jesus Christ?"

"I can't think of anything," she said.

"Would you do it now?"

"Yes." And there, in that moment, in the quietness of that dining room, she gave her life to Christ. That, for her, was God's hour.

There is a principle articulated in the New Testament which we must bear in mind with regard to our Christian witness and it goes as follows: "Some sow, some water, God giveth the increase." In your witness sometimes you will share your faith and that person will not make a commitment, but God has used you nonetheless—perhaps just to start that person thinking. You have witnessed and you have served God's purpose. It's just that you are not going to be around when all of that is fulfilled. Another person comes along perhaps days, weeks, months, or years later and says something else which waters the seed which you sowed and then God brings forth the increase. He brings that person to Himself.

That's the way it happened with Bill and I in that situation. The waitress initiated the conversation. (We don't always have to speak first.) He sowed the seed which caused her to go on thinking. And in the purpose of God it was my joy to water it and to see God bring forth the increase.

No one ever brings anyone to Christ really. God does that: that's the work of the Holy Spirit.

Chapter 7

Personal Evangelism: A Way of Life

"And the angel of the Lord spake unto Philip, saying, Arise, and go toward the south unto the way that goeth down from Jerusalem unto Gaza, which is desert.

"And he arose and went: and, behold, a man of Ethiopia, an eunuch of great authority under Candace the queen of the Ethiopians, who had charge of all her treasure, and had come to Jerusalem for to worship.

"Was returning, and sitting in his chariot read Esaias the prophet.

"Then the Spirit said unto Philip, go near, and join thyself to this chariot.

"And Philip ran thither to him, and heard him read the prophet Esaias, and said, Understandest thou what thou readest?

"And he said, How can I, except some man should guide me? And he desired Philip that he would come up and sit with him.

"The place of the Scripture which he read was

this, He was led as a sheep to the slaughter; and like a lamb dumb before his shearer, so opened he not his mouth:

"In his humiliation his judgment was taken away: and who shall declare his generation: for his life is taken from the earth.

"And the eunuch answered Philip, and said, I pray thee, of whom speaketh the prophet this? Of himself, or of some other man?

"Then Philip opened his mouth, and began at the same scripture and preached unto him Jesus.

"And as they went on their way, they came unto a certain water: and the eunuch said, See, here is water: What doth hinder me to be baptized?

"And Philip said, If thou believest with all thine heart, thou mayest. And he answered and said, I believe that Jesus Christ is the Son of God.

"And he commanded the chariot to stand still: and they went down both into the water, both Philip and the eunuch; and he baptized him.

"And when they were come up out of the water, the Spirit of the Lord caught away Philip, that the eunuch saw him no more: and he went on his way rejoicing" (Acts 8:26-39).

This remarkable story tells us the art of listening is important in personal evangelism. If we don't listen properly, we will find ourselves in the ridiculous position of creating more questions than we can answer or giving answers to unasked questions. The Ethiopian's inquiry ("Who is that the prophet is speaking about here: himself or someone else?") told Philip exactly what he needed to know—where he should start with this man. So he told him the good news of Jesus. Remember that this is what every sincere inquirer needs to hear—the good news of Jesus—the news of his own salvation made possible through the death of Christ on Calvary.

I cannot overemphasize this point—the necessity of always presenting the crucified and risen Lord to those who are in need of the abundant life. You will recall my mentioning earlier how this lesson was driven home to me in an unforgettable way. I had preached a sermon lacking this Gospel content and there was absolutely no public and visible response. The Bible sets the example as we see here in this story of Philip and the eunuch. We hear it again from the lips of Paul.

"When I came to you," he wrote to the Corinthians, "I declared the attested truth of God without display of fine words of wisdom. I resolved that while I was with you I would think of nothing but Jesus Christ—Christ nailed to the cross" (I Corinthians 2:2—NEB).

In evangelistic preaching, in group evangelism and in personal encounter, this is our message—there is no other. Jesus Christ crucified and risen.

There was immediate response to Philip's presentation of Jesus. "Look," said the eunuch, "here is water: what is there to prevent my being baptized?" Philip's sense of expectancy was self-evident. His own reaction, like that of all good fishermen, was to instantly pull in the net. But first, he challenged the seeker to profess Christ: "If you wholeheartedly believe, it is permitted." Having heard the profession, "I believe," Philip baptized him.

From beginning to end, this story demonstrates the leading role of the Holy Spirit in evangelism. Evangelists are simply instruments of His purpose, bound to obey His command, to follow His direction, to expound His word and to share His love.

It is difficult to believe that evangelism through personal encounter can be as simple as that of Philip and the Ethiopian eunuch. I was once troubled by what some call "instant Christianity." But now I see, as did Philip, that God can work His miracle of grace in such a simple fashion.

Only recently I was talking to an elderly man who suddenly asked if he could be confirmed. I asked if he was attending church.

"No," he said,"I don't go to any church. As a matter of fact, I haven't gone to church for more than fifty years." He then said something which made it very clear that he was both sincere in his inquiry and anxious about his spiritual state.

"I've got to get myself straightened out somehow. Perhaps you can help."

We met the following afternoon and his first question was, "What's this about being born again?"

"Where did you hear about being born again?"

"From my granddaughter," he said, "She says that unless I am born again, I won't enter heaven. Is that right? I have a friend who tells me the same thing and I hear Billy Graham say it on TV."

We started a simple Bible study to show him the essentials of the Christian faith. I avoided talking about rebirth—wanting to make certain he understood the need for such an experience. At the conclusion of that little study, I assigned some Bible reading with the understanding we would meet in two days.

The Holy Spirit continued to speak to him as he read God's Word and when we met at the appointed time, we completed a study of the good news of

Jesus Christ. His response, like that of the Ethiopian, was immediate.

"So that's what it is to be born again," he commented.

"It can happen to you," I said, "if you commit your life to Christ."

"That's what I'm here for," he replied.

I had absolutely no cause to doubt his sincerity, so we said a prayer of commitment. God heard his prayer, entered his life and did His wonderful work of grace. The proof of this was soon to be seen in his sincere, uninhibited sharing of Jesus Christ with his family and friends.

There are an amazing number of people ready to admit their need and anxious to learn what they have to do to be born again.

While visiting a minister and his wife, the conversation came around to the Christian faith. His wife, a woman in her late forties, suddenly said: "I don't know what you have I haven't got, but whatever it is, I want it."

I asked if she had accepted Christ. She replied, "No, and that's probably my problem, isn't it?"

When I had explained what it meant to have a personal encounter with Christ, she said, "I want to pray." To the amazement of her husband, she invited Christ to enter her life.

Billy Graham told the World Congress on Evangelism in Berlin how he led a taxi driver to Christ while he was being driven to the Congress hall.

My wife Joan was led to Christ by a friend of mine, a few weeks after he had met her.

Not all personal encounters are immediately productive. In many instances we may sow the seed while someone else in the future will have the joy of watering it and seeing God bring forth the increase. A strong sense of expectancy will not allow us to give way to disappointment on such occasions.

Two years ago, while conducting a crusade I was interviewed on a local radio station by a well-spoken young man. The taped interview lasted about an hour and gave me a terrific opportunity to articulate the Christian faith. Toward the end of the interview it was plain he had more than a passing curiosity. When the taping was complete, he shut off the recorder and said, "Do you have to leave now or can you spare some time?"

During the next hour, he sought answers to questions on the Gospel. He was married to a deeply committed Christian whose witness was having a profound effect on his life. It seemed to me this young man was ready to commit his life to Jesus Christ and perhaps he would have done so if another staff member had not been present in the adjoining room. He was reluctant to take the step at that moment but did promise to attend the crusade. Both he and his wife were present at most of the crusade services, but even then he failed to yield to the claims of Christ.

While I still don't know what happened to that man, I can't help but think that the witness of his wife (before I came along) and my testimony and answers had a positive effect on him. It may be that someone else—a total stranger—will eventually bring him to know the Lord. His wife and I may have to content ourselves with knowing we helped along the way.

The Christian ministry is more than a profession—it is a way of life. It is a life lived for

HIM, at all times and in all places. "For me to live is Christ" (Philippians 1:21). Because He is in us and we are in Him we cannot shed our ambassadorial role and garments as we encounter life apart from "religious" activities. This encounter, seen as a strong opportunity for evangelism and coupled with a keen sense of expectancy, makes the Christian life and ministry an exciting and breathtaking experience.

PART II

Chapter 8

Our Primary Task

The minister was called to fill in for a colleague at a hospital chapel service for the emotionally ill. He decided to deal with the purpose of life under the sermon title: "Why Are You Here?"

To immediately capture the attention of his restless chapel audience, he began his sermon by announcing his title with both clarity and authority: "Why Are You Here?" To make absolutely certain he had their undivided attention he said a second time: "Why Are You Here?" From the back of the chapel, with equal clarity and authority, came the answer: "Because we are not all there."

It is not for me to suggest you are not all there, but I do put the question:"Why are you here?" What is the purpose of your Christian life?

As a result of my ministry in North America and overseas, I am convinced that there are a staggering number of both laymen and ministers who cannot answer this question. They have either lost the sense of purpose in their lives and ministries, or never had it from the beginning. The result of such confusion is predictable—fruitless Christian lives and unproductive ministries. Countless souls not won for Christ for the simple reason that we do not know why we are here.

With the Church experiencing tremendous difficulties in winning a mid-twentieth-century world for Christ, we need to hear again those words of St. Paul, "If the trumpet gives an uncertain call, who will prepare himself to the battle?" (I Corinthians 14:8).

Why are **you** here? What is **your** primary task? I dare to ask such elementary questions even at the risk of insulting your intelligence and losing a reader. It is because these questions are so elementary that we tend to skip over them in our anxiety to get the job done. Then to our dismay we discover at some future date we really are not sure what the job is we are so anxious to complete.

Our primary reason for being here as Christians, laymen or pastors, is "to live for Christ" (Philippians 1:21) and in that living to exercise a ministry of reconciliation. "All things are of God," Paul writes, "who has reconciled us to himself by Jesus Christ, and has given unto **us** the ministry of reconciliation" (II Corinthians 5:18). This ministry of reconciliation is the primary task of every believer for we are all included in the "**us**"—every layman, every pastor. The purpose of **all** of our lives is "that we might by all means save some" (I Corinthians 9:22).

This ministry of reconciliation is supported by three pillars—without which we might well be believers but not power-filled witnesses, ministers but not evangelists. All three pillars—**prayer, power,** and

expectancy—command equal recognition.

PRAYER

The failure of a ministry of evangelism that does not begin and continue in prayer can be explained by the absence of that prayer. Without prayer, the ministry becomes our own, not His. If Christ does not own it, He does not bless it.

I believe that many Christians have no fruit in their lives because they do not ask. Do you, as a pastor, bother to ask God to bless your every visit in hospitals and homes? Do you, as a layman, bring before God the personal encounters that you will have this day in the course of your business and social life? Isn't it somewhat naive to believe that without prayer and without God's help, we will be sensitive, alert and responsive to the needs of the people in these situations? Letting the chips fall where they may, I find myself at times preparing my sermon, having started it without asking for His help to bring some measure of enlightenment, encouragement and instruction into the hearts of my congregation. Then I know it is time to start all over again—in prayer. The same principle applies to every phase of Christian living.

To neglect to commit our daily Christian lives and ministries to Him in prayer is just to go through the motions of being His ambassadors. It is inconceivable that any diplomatic ambassador would attempt to represent his president and government without regular consultation. We, as followers of Christ, serve the King of Kings. We are His representatives and ambassadors, and at all costs must therefore maintain the closest possible relationship with Him.

In daily consultation we can and must bring before Him in prayer those souls we would like to see reconciled to Him. How about the man I will be visiting in the hospital and the couple with marriage problems that I will be counselling? What about the man sitting at the desk next to me at the office? The neighbour with whom I will be having coffee later this morning—what of her spiritual needs?

This witnessing, this evangelism, as with all evangelism, begins on our knees. Let us name them in our prayers and thereby put flesh on our requests and then pray them into the family of God. For this purpose I highly recommend the use of a prayer notebook in which we record, as reminders, the names of those whom we are seeking to win to Christ.

POWER

All of us need to be reminded from time to time about the power that works in us. Our Lord's promise to His disciples at the time of His ascension applies as much to us in the twentieth century as it did to those in the first: "**You** shall receive **power** after the Holy Ghost has come upon you, and you shall be witnesses unto me" (Acts 1:8). Awareness of the presence and power of the Holy Spirit in one's life brings a new dimension to that life and its ministry of reconciliation. Surely it is this presence and power that sets the service of Christ, as a vocation, and as a way of life, apart from all others.

EXPECTANCY

The third pillar supporting the life and ministry of reconciliation is expectancy, something that is all too frequently absent in the lives of Christians, even in the most evangelical circles.

In the beginning of my itinerant evangelistic ministry, I held a crusade in a small church in Western Canada. I asked the minister for a room where we could counsel those who responded to the Gospel message each evening. His suggestion was a room which at best would accommodate three people. This obviously wasn't good enough and I had to ask for something else. It turned out the church basement had ample room for thirty-five chairs. On the first evening we needed thirteen chairs and before the week was out, all but a few of the thirty-five seats. That minister (a very godly man) felt sufficiently moved to reassess **his** sense of expectancy.

During a crusade ministry in the Orient, I met many pastors, strong evangelicals, who like many of their North American counterparts had lost their sense of expectancy. Japanese ministers and foreign missionaries cautioned me that Orientals, because of their shyness, could not be expected to openly respond to the Gospel. They were also convinced that the faith needed to be taught over a long period of time before Orientals could be expected to make a personal commitment.

I told them I didn't believe that such a position could be supported in the New Testament. I was unhappy about being brought thousands of miles to preach the Gospel only to discover that as a fisherman I was not to be permitted to pull in the net. To me, this was a most unusual way to fish. But because I was a foreigner I was reluctant to tell my hosts what to do and I agreed to preach Christ and forego the invitation or altar call.

On the evening of the first service I was praying

with my Japanese interpreter, Koji Hayashi. When we finished I said, "Koji, my spirit is deeply bothered by this turn of events. How can I preach Christ and not invite my listeners to accept Him?"

"Marney," he said, "I believe you are right and they are wrong." This was all I needed to hear. One of their own number had agreed with me and I accepted this as a clear direction from the Lord.

"Koji," I said, "hurry! Call another meeting of the pastors and crusade committee." It was less than fifteen minutes before the commencement of the service.

A few minutes later a perplexed group of ministers and laymen heard me saying that my spirit was very unhappy about our agreement not to have an invitation following the nightly messages.

"I would like to strike a bargain with you," I said. "Tonight, let me do it my way, based on my experience. If there is no response from the people, we will do it your way for the other nights." They agreed. That night the Holy Spirit did His miraculous work in the hearts of the people and lives were transformed in numbers far exceeding anything yet experienced in my ministry.

It began on the first night and before the three crusades were finished, over 35 percent of the audience had responded to the Good News of Jesus Christ.

Letters from Japanese pastors and missionaries who witnessed this wonderful work of God testify to the continued growth in the faith of many of those who gave their lives to Christ in those days and subsequently were baptized.

These two incidents surely serve to remind all of us, laity and pastors alike, that we are fishermen in the fullest sense of the word. When a fisherman sets out, he fully expects to be successful and is equipped with a net. My wife and I went on a fishing trip this summer, and shortly after our departure, discovered that we had neglected to pack our net. At some inconvenience and loss of time, we returned to our camp site to secure it. Why? Because we fully expected we would need it. After all, were we not going hoping, indeed expecting, to bring home some fish? We must likewise always anticipate—expect— success in our fishing for men. Has He not promised that as we share His Holy Word in our fishing "it shall not return unto (Him) empty"?

> For as the rain cometh down, and the snow from heaven, and returneth not thither, but watereth the earth, and maketh it bring forth and bud that it may give seed to the sower, and bread to the eater: so shall my word be that goeth forth out of my mouth: **it shall not return unto me empty**, but it shall accomplish that which I please, and it shall **prosper** in the thing whereunto I sent it.

(Isaiah 55:10-11)

Believe this to be literally true. **Memorize it, graft it** into your heart and mind, then witness to Christ expectantly; share Him, preach Him, and you will find yourself living continually in the realm of the miracle where individuals in increasing numbers experience a personal encounter with the living God.

Chapter 9

Opportunities Abound!

The first thing he said when I entered his hospital room was, "I'm an atheist." I had seen him two or three times as he was numbered among the C.E. crowd (not Church of England but Christmas and Easter). Now he was seriously ill and very much on the defensive.

On occasions such as this, only the Holy Spirit can provide the appropriate words and the proper measure of grace with which to say them.

"Are you happy being an atheist?" His mouth dropped ever so slightly and his eyebrows raised to crease his forehead—involuntary reflexes disclosing his surprise at the frankness of my question. For a moment he hesitated. "No," he replied, "I'm not."

"Tell me about it," I said. "When did you become an atheist?"

"In the 8th Army in Egypt. If I believed anything before that time, I certainly lost it in the sands of the western desert."

An hour later he was still talking about war

experiences. It became obvious that he was more of an agnostic seeker than an atheist, for he felt in his heart that while there must be a God, His existence could not be proven. On the other hand, he dearly wanted to believe that such a God did exist. Using this as a starting point, I told him a little of the Gospel story. Not wanting to give him spiritual indigestion I said I would return in the immediate future.

As I was leaving, I reached into my pocket and felt a little book. It was a paperback copy of John's Gospel. I left it on the bed and said, "Read it, if you have the time. You'll find it very interesting."

"I have all kinds of time," he said. "I'm here for at least a month."

When I returned, I asked if he'd read the booklet. "Yes," was his reply, "I read the entire book."

"Did you find it helpful?" Again the answer was affirmative.

"What was the main thing you learned from reading the Gospel?"

"Well, for one thing," he said, "to enter heaven I must be born again!"

He was born again that very hour, as he sincerely committed his life to Christ. And so it was that this battle-hardened veteran found a new way of life as the Holy Spirit spoke to him through God's Holy Word.

> "As the rain and the snow come down from heaven and do not return until they have watered the earth, making it blossom and bear fruit, and give seed for sowing and bread to eat, so shall the Word which comes from my mouth prevail; it shall **not** return to me

fruitless without accomplishing My
purpose or succeeding in the task I gave
it."

Isaiah 55:10,11 (NEB)

LITERATURE

This experience underlines the importance of our
always having appropriate literature available.
Before entering the hospital for my first visit with
this "atheist" I had been prompted to reach into the
glove compartment of my car for the copy of John's
Gospel, which is surely the most appropriate
literature for any believer to carry with him. By
"appropriate" I mean that which is written for a
particular or special purpose, which, of course, is the
case with John's Gospel. "These are written that ye
might believe that Jesus is the Christ, the Son of
God; and that believing ye might have life through
his name" (John 20:31).

Unknown to me, the Holy Spirit was already at
work, prior to my visit, preparing the heart of that
man for the sowing of the seed of God's word—a
seed which I had been led to carry in my car and on
my person for precisely this reason, and which He
now used to accomplish His purpose in the life of the
seeker.

A frequent spot-check of one's pocket, purse,
briefcase, or glove compartment can serve to avoid
the loss of opportunities in using literature in the
sharing of the Gospel. The following experience
comes to mind as I write these words.

While attending the American Congress on
Evangelism, I had dinner with a long-standing
friend. Our waitress was a vivacious young lady who
was a second-year philosophy student from

Minneapolis. During the dinner I became increasingly aware of the leading of the Holy Spirit. When she returned to serve coffee, I asked about her college course and how her various subjects corresponded with her religious convictions. She said she wasn't quite sure about the nature of her convictions but she had been reared in a Lutheran home. I asked if she believed in a personal God who cared about her and her needs. She replied in the negative.

"Would you **like** to believe there is a God who cares for you?" I asked.

"Oh yes, very much."

I reached for my usual literature only to discover it wasn't there. While I continued talking, my assistant hurried to my hotel room and returned eight or ten minutes later with the appropriate material.

I know she didn't come to Christ at that time, but the seed was sown and having literature available played an important role. While it was a trifle embarrassing not to have the literature I needed right there in my pocket, what would have happened to her or the effectiveness of my witnessing if none had been available? Would a fisherman go to sea without the net, hooks or gaff? We are fishers of men!

From the thousands of booklets available, we can choose those most appropriate to our individual tastes. It pays to be selective; it is essential to choose that with which we are most comfortable and which we can use without apology.

For years I have been carrying two booklets in my pocket and car—a paperback copy of John's Gospel produced by Scripture Gift Mission and a commentary on John's Gospel produced by Scripture

Union entitled **Invitation to Live**. These are two mighty weapons which God has used many times in my own witnessing.

VISITATION

Most pastors, and praise God an increasing number of dedicated laymen, allot a considerable amount of time for visiting people in hospital and home. This is a very good use of time, provided our motives are in proper perspective. While such visits, as well as other phases of parish ministry, should be included in the area known as "feeding the flock," the visitation ministry exercised by laymen and pastors is also an unexcelled opportunity to bring people to Christ.

Who do we visit and for what purpose? To what extent are pastoral visits designed to maintain the "status quo," to keep up attendance (and the offering) and to keep the church board happy? It's the sad truth that many people today see ministers more as authorities on the weather, tea and coffee than as ambassadors for Christ. By our own omissions we have succeeded in creating an image of the ministry of the church which leaves a tremendous amount to be desired and which makes it increasingly difficult for us to have a parish visitation program where we share with people "that which we have seen and heard."

The pastor's or layman's visit, properly understood and undertaken, can be one of the most productive areas of his ministry. But the visitor must make up his mind that his visits are going to centre on the **spiritual** needs of the people. Once this is established, then he can seek the daily guidance of the Holy Spirit as he plans and carries out his visits to meet those spiritual needs.

COUNSELLING

The same principle applies to the counselling ministry which today is making ever-increasing demands on the life of both the pastor and the committed and dedicated layman. In one year, near the end of my parish ministry, I had 387 interviews in which I counselled people anticipating marrage, people whose marriages were not succeeding, people who were inquiring about baptism and confirmation and people with problems covering virtually every area of human experience. Each interview represented, in varying degrees, a golden opportunity to present the Person of Christ. Not all those I counselled were brought to Him, but some did recognize their need for a new dimension in life. When they learned that Christ offered this, they committed their lives to Him. The validity of their commitment is clearly seen in the worshipping and witnessing patterns which developed in their lives.

While I am not suggesting we can have a batting average of a thousand in our counselling ministry, I am saying that in every serious counselling interview we must make every effort to present Jesus Christ as the Way, the Truth and the Life, without Whom no man can come to God.

The fruitfulness of our visitation and counselling ministry is closely related to other areas of our lives where we also proclaim Jesus Christ. There can be dozens of contributing factors in the conversion of an individual. The initial seed may be planted through a Sunday sermon, through something said in a Bible study or during a casual personal encounter with a neighbour, fellow worker or friend. This seed is sometimes watered in a counselling session and God brings forth the increase.

It's the little pieces fitting together to form the completed masterpiece. I remember one incident in which I played a tape of Bishop Chandu Ray's testimony for a small group at the church. Bishop Ray had given this testimony thousands of miles away at the World Congress on Evangelism in Berlin.

A few days after hearing the tape, a young lady called and wanted to talk. She later gave her heart to the Lord Jesus Christ and is now in full-time service.

On another occasion, the seed was sown in a Bible study. A young mother talked to me after the class. I asked her if she knew Christ. She said "yes," but with real hesitancy. She was talking to me some time later: "I kept asking myself, 'What makes me think I know Christ? Why did I say yes?' It was then I realized I didn't know Him at all and I really wanted to experience His love."

Arriving home and finding her husband asleep, she sat in the darkness and quietness of her living room and a short time later knelt and gave her life to Christ.

This sense of expectancy is an attitude which must be reflected throughout all of our ministry all of the time—in the pulpit, in hospital visits, in parish visiting on Tuesday and Bible class on Wednesday, and in every area of the committed layman's life. The extent to which this is true will determine the fruitfulness of our lives.

Chapter 10

Household Fellowships: Coffee Cup Evangelism

In the life of the Church today there is great need for experimentation. Under God we must constantly try new ways of communicating the Gospel of Jesus Christ to the ever-expanding community of unbelievers. The Household Fellowship ministry has been just such an experiment for us in our Invitation to Live Crusades.

When explaining this ministry I begin with the title, saying it is much more than a title—it is a philosophy. The name "Household Fellowship" was deliberately chosen for what it does **not** say. I believe we have a very real problem in the Christian Church today that we must recognize and deal with if we expect any success in grass roots evangelism.

Nowhere is this more evident than in the titles we use for various groups that are intended to be evangelistic. How many times do ministers complain about the increasing lack of interest in prayer meetings and Bible Study groups? I have heard many ministers try to account for the problem of waning interest in mid-week prayer meetings. It's our affluent society some say. Others attribute it to the increasing apathy of church members—they're just not interested in meeting for Bible Study and prayer anymore! There is probably some measure of truth in all of this, but part of the problem is also ours—the ministers'. We are attacking the world of the 20th century with 19th century methods.

Two things are necessary. We must make a clear distinction between feeding the flock of God with the teaching ministry (The New Testament didachē) and the proclamation of the Gospel (the kerygma).

We must also use terms suitable to the occasion and relevant to the times. The terms "prayer meeting" and "Bible Study group" have been used as far back as any of us can remember. There is no need to discard them in the modern world of the 20th century if they still meet a need—that is, if people continue to attend such groups. There may have been occasions in the past when unbelievers were found in many of these groups, although I seriously doubt in any large numbers. Such is not the case today. The only relationship the unbeliever has to such groups is that he is conspicuous by his absence.

It is naive to suggest, as many do, that the Bible is of no interest to the vast majority of people. Just look at the ever-increasing sales of Bibles and Testaments. Never has the Bible been so much in demand, especially in such practical and exciting versions as **Good News for Modern Man** and **The Living Bible**. We must ask ourselves, who and what really are the problems?

The **who** of the problem is **us**—ministers of the Gospel. We cling tenaciously to old terms and old methods, proclaiming them to be virtues. And the world passes us by. But for Christ and for people in the 20th century, the past is not good enough. Praise God for the fact that an increasing number of His ministers are finally beginning to recognize this fact.

The **what** of the problem is one of terminology. We insist on using terms, words and titles which are part of our theological jargon. But these words have very little meaning for those outside of the faith (and for many who are in the faith). I question the value of using titles such as "prayer meeting" and "Bible Study group" if we are trying to reach unbelievers for Christ. Even if we endeavor to use such activities to "feed the flock of God," surely we can come up with more original titles which are as meaningful and far more relevant. You might want to try "The Pastor's Hour," "The Carpenter's Union," or "Christian Faith Inquiry Class."

Since the purpose of the Household Fellowship is to bring the participants to a saving knowledge of Jesus Christ, this brings us to the **how** of the matter—the approach or method.

I begin by explaining how the Fellowships are organized.

PERSONNEL

We don't need or want leaders in the groups in the normal sense of the word. What we do need are deeply committed, mature Christians who have the gifts of love, wisdom, patience and diplomacy. They are not leaders but moderators. The difference is that a leader directs while the moderator **guides** discussion. The last person you want as moderator is the one with all the answers and a compulsion to enunciate them. The group should be searching and seeking and listening. The moderator's task is to provide every assistance. Sometimes a husband and wife fill this role and where possible, this is most desirable. It is sometimes necessary to use a man or woman and I'll risk being called chauvinistic to suggest that the man be moderator.

When the moderator is selected, you need a husband-and-wife team to act as host and hostess. Their three duties are simple but important. They offer their home for ninety minutes a week over a certain period of time. They should be willing to serve coffee or tea (nothing more) to those attending. Finally, they should be willing to assist the moderator to invite people from the neighbourhood to attend the Fellowships.

ORGANIZING THE GROUP

The natural place to begin is with the "known"—those on the church list the minister knows are **uncommitted** to Christ. Added to these are the families in the community whom the host, hostess, or moderator knows are still seeking Christ.

These folks are invited by the host couple or moderator to attend a fellowship on a specific night. It is understood that they are invited to attend this one meeting and for a time not to exceed one hour. (It is best to start at 8:00 p.m., and conclude at 9:00 p.m.) The time factor is important as some people will have arranged for a baby-sitter. If they know it involves an hour and not an entire evening, they are more apt to attend.

The invitation states you are inviting a number of couples to your home for a brief time of fellowship and discussion. If the couple wants further information, explain the purpose in detail. Mention that you are hoping to have an interesting time discussing various aspects of the Christian faith. Mention that this will involve only lay people—"it's among ourselves"—for no ministers are to be present in these groups. It is very helpful if you can say your particular reason for holding such a meeting is in preparation for a church anniversary, crusade or mission.

Invitations are extended until a minimum of three couples and a maximum of four have accepted. The moderator and spouse and the host and hostess make up a further two couples for a maximum attendance of twelve. Experience has taught us that at least eight people are needed to make a group function well and that twelve is a maximum if all are to participate.

THE FELLOWSHIP FORMAT

Your guests may arrive anywhere from fifteen minutes before the agreed time up until the last minute. Man the coffee pot! Serve coffee or tea immediately upon arrival—after each couple has been introduced to those present. I cannot stress too strongly the importance of serving a beverage at this time—**prior** to the beginning of the fellowship. It serves to "break the ice" and provides a vehicle for casual conversation, all of which creates a warm, informal atmosphere before the group convenes. Care should be taken not to serve food at this time. To do so creates unnecessary work and expense for the hosts, and little, if anything, is achieved.

When all guests have arrived and coffee has been served, it's over to the moderator. Exactly on the hour—for the time is important—the moderator casually convenes the group by mentioning he is delighted so many could come.He could thank the host and hostess for opening their home and should then explain as briefly as possible the purpose of the meeting.

He might say something like this: "As we have already mentioned to some of you, our main purpose is to provide an opportunity to get to know one another and talk about the Christian faith. We are only one of many such groups meeting across the city for the same purpose.

"We have an hour and I'd suggest, for a beginning, that we talk about prayer and what we should pray for, and then spend a little time looking through (don't say studying) the Bible to see what we can learn about the Christian faith. In other words, we are going to search together to see what we can learn and what we can do with what we learn...the application of it.

"Let's begin by thinking about prayer, just for a moment or two. What are some of the things we ought to pray about?"

The more obvious things are always suggested. Peace in the world, the sick, the unemployed, the bereaved, our neighbours, our family and friends. The purpose of this exercise is to draw out the group. Receiving its suggestions forms the basis for a time of prayer which now follows. The moderator continues...

"We now have some excellent ideas for prayer and I suggest we do just that. Let's pray about these matters, but in so doing remember these simple guidelines. No one should feel he **has** to pray; so now you can relax."

Some are going to do just that because for a moment they wanted to run for the door.

"And when you do pray, say it in two sentences or less."

Those who previously had mentally elected not to participate now see the possibility to do so without losing face. (If I can't say one sentence, something is wrong with me!) The main intention of this approach is to make it so simple that everyone feels, "I can do this!"

This basic rule for prayer participation immediately discourages the person with previous experience in extemporaneous praying (the one who can pray about the world and its problems for fifteen minutes without drawing a breath.)

It is an important rule because the inexperienced person, as most of the group should be, will feel spiritually inferior in the company of such a "talented" and "spiritual" person. The newcomer cannot help but conclude that this "just isn't my piece of cake." For this person, the entire purpose of the meeting is lost. In most cases this situation will not arise if a deliberate attempt has been made to invite non-church attenders and non-believers.

"Let's just do that for a moment or two, shall we? Let's bow our heads and you pray as you feel like it. At the end of your prayer simply say, "amen" so we'll know your prayer is finished. Then we will say "amen" after you. We can pray about any of the things that have been mentioned or anything else."

The next few minutes are for some the most gratifying and thrilling spiritual experience of their lives. Much to their amazement they find themselves praying aloud in the company of others for the first time. Anyone who can recall the first time he prayed in this manner will remember his own excitement and joy arising out of the experience.

If any of my readers are skeptical at this point about the success of this approach to prayer, you are not alone. I was very skeptical when I heard a friend suggest it to a group of parishioners. He concluded his talk saying: "Now, let's join in some sentence prayers." Under my breath I said, "Lots of luck, brother!"

I seriously doubted anyone would participate. But most of them did pray and that remained a lesson in spiritual skepticism and human understanding that I trust I'll never forget. I could not count the ministers and laity in numerous communities where we have had crusades who testify that this approach is one which God does use in the lives of those who seek Him.

The period of prayer should last no more than six or seven minutes. Sometimes there are questions or comments on the prayers and it may be necessary to limit such conversation to get on with the next part of the fellowship. It's quite important that they participate in a complete fellowship so they can evaluate it and decide whether or not to participate in future groups.

The moderator then explains the procedure for Bible discussion. The approach must be very casual and informal. Above all, avoid those well known, sterile and rigid instruction periods. We suggest something like this to introduce this phase of the fellowship...

"Let's go to the other part of our evening discussion about the Christian faith. As a basis for our discussion, I suggest we read a few verses of Scripture."

Paperback versions of either **Good News for Modern Man,** a New Testament in modern English, or single copies of a Gospel in a modern translation are distributed.

I should explain another ground rule for Household Fellowships. No one brings a Bible to these groups. This immediately creates the image of a typical church-run Bible class. Many of those present, having difficulty locating a particular book in the Bible, get embarrassed and ill at ease. The distribution of a single Gospel or New Testament solves such problems.

The moderator proceeds by saying, "Let's turn to page one—and you'll find the first chapter of Luke."

Individual copies of the Gospels are preferred as they deal directly with the life and teachings of Christ and are usually available without cost from Scripture Gift Mission or other agencies.

Page one is no problem for anyone. The group reads in unison a given number of verses chosen by the moderator. Reading aloud and together avoids embarrassment associated with inability to pronounce certain words and helps the individual to overcome the apprehension associated with hearing the sound of his own voice.

The moderator can then say: "Good! Now let's go back to the first verse and see what it says to us. It may say different things to different people. Who wants to comment?"

Normally, someone has something to say about the verse and may see and understand a new truth. Questions about the verse should be discussed by the group under the moderator's supervision.

If there are no questions or comments on the first verse, the moderator moves on until the entire passage has been discussed verse by verse.

Some will question this particular approach to Bible

study, saying it is necessary to have a minister present who will provide answers to questions raised in the group. I do not feel it is always necessary to have such a person present when the Bible is being studied by a group. I draw support for this position from both the New Testament and personal experience.

Our Lord admonished us to "search" the Scriptures (John 5:39) and He makes no mention of the necessity of having a qualified pastor present. Can anyone seriously doubt that the worship of the early Christians in their small "house churches" (Romans 16:5; I Corinthians 4:15; Colossians 4:15) included the study of God's Holy Word?

During my time in the pastorate and in mass evangelism, I have seen many, many people come to Christ through reading God's Holy Word. When ministering to the Eskimos in our Arctic crusades, I sometimes almost forgot that many of these people had been without the benefit of weekly church services and the guidance of a trained minister for long periods of time. But they had spiritually grown by faithfully reading the Word of God.

A friend of mine committed his life to Christ after reading two follow-up booklets I had sent to his wife after her own conversion. It's about time we pastors let go of our laity. Give the Holy Spirit freedom of movement! Who are we to deny this to our charges?

The discussion period in the Household Fellowship continues until five minutes before the hour. The moderator can close with a comment such as, "That's what a Household Fellowship is all about. Just a little time of prayer and the reading of the Bible as a basis for discussing the Christian faith. Groups like this are meeting in other parts of town.

The idea is to establish this kind of fellowship where there is sufficient interest on a continuing basis.

"We promised not to keep you more than the hour and our time is almost up. If you want to meet on a weekly basis, we can meet here—thanks to Mr. and Mrs. (Jones) (host and hostess). If you want time to think it over, fine, but who would like to come next week?"

The show of hands provides a clear indication of interest in what until now had been a one-time experiment. It's a rare case when there isn't sufficient interest to continue the group. Some couples want to discuss it between themselves, but there are always a few couples who make up their minds right away that this is for them and they want to meet the group again. If this is the case, two questions should be resolved:

1) Which evening is convenient for most of the group? Should there be a change?

2) What about the most convenient hour?

After these two questions are resolved, the moderator can close the fellowship...

"OK, for those who would like to come, we'll meet again next Wednesday at 8:00 p.m."

The choice of staying for further fellowship is left to individual couples. Pressure to stay longer should be avoided because time is very important to some couples.

It's possible for a Household Fellowship to successfully function with only six or eight people, although a group of six can be a little difficult if one or two individuals are shy or withdrawn. The personalities of those in the smaller groups make or break the success of the group. The group can start with the host and hostess, the moderator and spouse, and one or two other couples. In due course, others may quite naturally find their way into the fellowship. Don't be discouraged by numbers. Our Lord began with two men before adding others. When He was finished, He had selected only twelve. Those few men who believed in Christ and grew in faith through their fellowship with Him and one another went out and turned the world upside down!

It is our hope that the committed and mature members of the Household Fellowship will eventually be led by the Holy Spirit to go out, two by two, to establish further groups, reproducing their own kind—for as Christians we are born to reproduce.

Chapter 11

Mass Evangelism:
Talking To Ourselves?

Mass evangelism is many things to many people. For some it means an evangelistic crusade or mission. For others, preaching the Gospel of Christ on television or radio. Others see it as the widest possible distribution of Christian literature. Mass evangelism can be any or all of these, for the objective is always the same—to share the Good News of Jesus Christ at the same time with large numbers of people.

The kind of mass evangelism I am most familiar with is the crusade. Many crusade ministries, my own included, can and do use some or all of the above-mentioned methods.

The evangelistic crusade, which concentrates on proclaiming the Gospel to an assembled crowd, is a ministry found in Holy Scripture. It began with our Lord. He, on more than one occasion, spoke to large numbers of people.

When discussing the crusade, I make a clear

distinction between a service for committed people and the evangelistic crusade which has as its primary objective the winning of unbelievers to Christ. This distinction avoids any confusion in planning and preparation. Failure to make such a distinction not only results in confusion in the preparation and program, but yields bitter disappointment in the results.

I've seen too many crusades which were intended to be evangelistic but turned out to be nothing more than services of Christian witness. The audiences were comprised of those who knew the Gospel and what it meant to be converted. This is not evangelism—it is just talking to ourselves. Evangelism has never taken place and never will take place when Christians talk to themselves. As evangelists, we must make absolutely sure that our planning and preparation teams will guarantee us an audience with a large number of unbelievers. Failure to provide such an audience nullifies any sense of expectancy in the heart of the preacher. It brings dishonour to the Holy Spirit whose work of transformation is not evident in the response to the invitation. And that response, if it takes place at all, clearly indicates the evangelist has been talking to himself for thirty to forty minutes.

I recently attended what was publicized as an evangelistic crusade. A very able evangelist was the speaker. As the people streamed into the building, my heart went out to the man who was to preach the unsearchable riches of Christ. I knew that at the conclusion of his message he would issue an invitation to respond to the Gospel. I also knew beforehand it would be virtually in vain. I knew, from that audience of 4,000, very few would step forward. WHY?

Didn't he preach the Gospel? Yes, he preached it with clarity and great conviction. Why then would there be little response? Because unbelievers don't carry a Bible to a public meeting. On that occasion, those not carrying Bibles could be counted on the fingers of two hands. The failure, then, was clearly the responsibility of the crusade committee which had neglected in its planning to make a clear distinction between an evangelistic crusade and a service of witness. This oversight lost both the committee and the evangelist the kind of audience they sincerely wanted to reach. Their intentions were the very best. Their program of planning and preparation to attract the unbeliever left a tremendous amount to be desired. The unbeliever was conspicuous by his absence.

The success of any crusade or mission is contingent not on the persuasive ability and dynamic personality of any evangelist, but rather on the ministers, the laity, and the evangelist being workers together with Him.

In working together with Him, they must have a clearly defined objective which must show in all their planning and preparation. The objective of any evangelistic enterprise is to evangelize—to bring people into a personal encounter with the living Christ. All planning must focus on that single objective. To achieve that objective, preparations must draw the unbeliever's attention to the event (the crusade). Then you win his interest. And then you make it easy and convenient for him to attend.

For the unbeliever to be won to Christ he must come under the sound of the Gospel, a sound he will not hear if he is not in attendance. His attendance is the main responsibility of the organizing committee. The message he will hear—the Gospel—is the concern of the evangelist. If both committee and evangelist do their work prayerfully and under the guidance of the Holy Spirit, He will bring forth the increase.

Space does not permit a full discussion of all the aspects of the crusade ministry—but certain salient features do need special attention.

PRAYER

The power behind mass evangelism and all evangelism is prayer—continual, faithful prayer offered by God's people on behalf of an evangelistic project. The net result of all evangelism depends more on prayer than any other single factor. The very first job of the organizing committee is to get God's people praying for the crusade. How?

Encourage more people to remember the crusade in their daily devotions.

They can pray together on Sunday.

The various groups which meet throughout the week as a part of the activity of the church should be encouraged to support the crusade in prayer.

Special prayer groups should be formed as part of the prayer force behind the crusade.

There are other ways to enlist prayer support. Before one of our crusades in California, 300 people were praying over the telephone, asking God to bless our ministry in their midst. It was a simple and imaginative idea—certain people started each day by calling other designated prayer partners. The caller led in a brief prayer followed by a responding prayer taken by the party who received the call, who then made another call, following the same procedure.

Three hundred prayer partners praying daily! Little wonder we commenced that crusade with a real sense of expectancy!

PUBLICITY

Hand in hand with prayer goes publicity. Think of them as two sides of a coin—praying as though everything depends upon God and publicizing as though everything depends upon us. There is mighty power in prayer—without it, all is in vain. But I also know we must use every available means to win the attention of today's secular world. Publicity is a regrettable-but-necessary aspect of any form of mass evangelism. We must constantly pray for a full measure of humility when we find ourselves as the focus of attention in such publicity.

DELEGATIONS

I want to include in my comments on the work of the crusade committee a few observations on the importance of delegations. The wide use of delegations assures maximum attendance. Our experience has shown it represents the best medium to reach the maximum number of unbelievers.

In preparation for a crusade, we ask each minister and lay leader to provide a written list of every group and club (religious and secular) known to him in the crusade area. If possible we get the leader's name and address.

These lists are processed and followed up by the delegations committee. A double-check ensures that every existing organization and group is included—from the firemen and the badminton club to the town council and the PTA. Even if some people just meet regularly or have some common bond such as working together, they should be encouraged to attend the crusade as a group.

All this tiring footwork is essential because you'll often find that such groups contain large numbers of people who have no church connection and would have little reason, if any, to attend an evangelistic crusade.

In one of our crusades, some years ago, a woman who once worked in the town clerk's office was in charge of delegations. She was very well acquainted with the affairs of the community of some 3,000 people and as a result of the dedication and hard work of her committee, eighty-six groups were invited to attend. The crusade building was packed to overflowing each evening. On some occasions more than sixty percent of the seats were reserved for the delegations. Of those who responded to the Gospel in that crusade, a large number came from the delegations whose attendance was made possible and encouraged by the work of a very dedicated committee.

USHERS

The principle of involving the unchurched also applies to our ushers. We don't recruit them from church ushering committees. We go after those who don't regularly attend church. They are usually quite happy to help and they take their responsibilities seriously. Our philosophy is that by being in attendance, they hear the Gospel. In a small-town crusade, we might have as many as 125 ushers—when twelve would be more than adequate. More than a few have been known to give their lives to Christ.

UMBRELLA OUTREACH

In making plans for an evangelistic crusade or mission, remember that the public services should represent only one phase of the overall program. Properly used, a crusade can be a very large umbrella under which a host of evangelistic activities take place quite apart from the main service. A community-wide crusade can be the vehicle which opens doors at high schools, universities, service clubs, offices and factories.

During our northern Japan crusades in 1969, the Christian manager of a large chemical company arranged for me to address all his employees (most were Buddhist) in the company cafeteria. Their undivided attention and keen interest gave ample testimony to the effectiveness of such an outreach.

In that same city the Christian principal of a girls' high school invited me to speak to 1,200 students. Even though most of them were Buddhist, many later attended crusade services. From all the reports we received, we know that a large number of those students had a personal experience of Christ, made possible in part by our first contact with them in the high school auditorium.

EXPECTANCY AND IMAGINATION

My contention is that we must be both expectant and imaginative in our approach to mass evangelism, praying always that God will give us the wisdom to understand the world we seek to win, the courage to confront it with the Gospel and a sense of expectancy when we do.

There are those who protest that the day of mass evangelism is over. I say it has yet to begin. We minister in the age of the masses, when two and a half million people are added to the world's population every ten days. It is a competitive age in which the prize is the soul of man. To win that prize the Church must use the very finest of personnel and use every means at its disposal—one of which is mass evangelism. As our world population continues to explode unchecked, a new day has dawned in the life of the Church. It is a day in which mass evangelism in all its forms must and will play a leading role.

Chapter 12

The Spiritual Climate

A prerequisite for an evangelistic ministry is a spiritual climate. In-depth evangelism means the consistent winning of people to Jesus Christ—and there must be a certain spiritual atmosphere if this is to take place. This atmosphere, believe me, does not come automatically.

I suppose every minister has had the experience where preaching to a congregation seemed like preaching to a walk-in freezer. It also happens at crusades. Yes, in spite of people and planning, it is possible to bypass the Spirit of God.

When the Spirit of God is not present, we who serve Him know. And we know that there is nothing so discouraging in the Christian ministry as to know that God is not present. The result of such a ministry is predictable...little if any fruit.

The most important committee in any crusade, mission or parish is the Prayer Committee. The Prayer Committee's responsibility is to harness the prayer life of the people in support of the ministry.

We must keep things in their proper perspective. We work in His ministry—not ours. Our work is not of man, but of God and without Him "we can do nothing."

The same spiritual principle applies to the whole of the Christian life and ministry. As individuals, we should certainly pray about our personal witness. And surely any parish ministry must be supported by prayer, even if that prayer is offered only by a small nucleus of faithful people. Never forget that we have His promise "wherever two or three are gathered together in My name, there am I in the midst of them." It wouldn't hurt to remember from time to time that it was the unceasing prayers of a comparatively small group, meeting in the house of Mary, that brought about the release of Peter from the Roman prison.

Yes, "many more things are wrought of God through prayer than any man dreams of...." It is this faithful, expectant prayer that serves to provide much of the spiritual climate in which the Holy Spirit can most readily transform the lives of those who hear the Gospel.

The prayerful support of any ministry begins with the man himself. Concerning the clergy, many of the laity are inclined to take this for granted, feeling that to be a minister of God is to be a man of prayer. While we ministers might wish this were the case, we know that all too often it isn't. I believe this is one of the central problems in the Church. It is a problem which has to be met square on by every theological college and seminary. If a minister fails to keep his ministry before God, through a disciplined prayer life, what then can he expect, much less request, of his laity?

There is a story about an Anglican bishop who was to take a confirmation service in one of the more successful parishes in his Diocese. This church was moving ahead at a great pace—meeting its large budget, experiencing rapid growth and presenting a large number of candidates for confirmation. It certainly seemed to be a parish which was spiritually on fire and the bishop looked forward to his visit. He was anxious to meet this young, new clergyman whose ministry was capturing everyone's attention. He fully expected to meet a young man who was aggressive, a gifted preacher and a real organizer. Instead, he found a man of prayer, a man with a disciplined devotional life who consulted His Lord about everything and anything—a man who walked with God.

How close is your walk with the Lord?

Sometimes we ministers are more inclined to enunciate a problem than to offer solutions. I have evolved what I believe to be some practical, personal suggestions for a person's devotional life.

I always use a prayer notebook. It's my spiritual ignition key, the source of power in my ministry. Through it, the Power is turned on—a Power which manifests itself in every situation and project. Using this little aid puts flesh on my prayer life, for it always involves people...their problems, their sufferings, their aspirations and their joys.

I have a page for those who are ill. It is easy to keep it up-to-date every day. Isn't it so easy to say "I'll pray for you" and just as easy to forget? What a difference it makes to be able to sincerely say to a parishioner in hospital: "I'm remembering you in prayer." And what encouragement this provides to those who are ill when they know this to be true!

I keep another page or two for those with special troubles...things like marriage problems, unemployment, alcoholism or the pains of youth. Do you pray for your own responsibilities? My list includes preparing and preaching sermons, lectures, Bible class, the Sunday School teachers' meetings, the finance committee meeting....

Shouldn't all of these and more be a very real part of one's prayer life? I try to pray such that there is a spiritual climate in evidence from the sound of the gavel. How many activities are there in the life of the average church where the first prayer is said after the meeting is convened?

No pastor can carry the full responsibility of prayer support for the ministry of any church. But it begins with him, the man himself. Then and only then can he honestly solicit the support of his people.

What about the laity? In every congregation there are always those few fully committed and converted people who are deeply devoted to the service of Christ and His Church. Pastor, here is your parish power-house! Draw those faithful souls into a fellowship of concern. Acquaint them with the needs of the church and your needs and aspirations. You should be able to count on them to remember next week's annual meeting of the congregation, the election of officers, or the fact that two new teachers are needed in the church school. Prayerful people can be informed of the sermon topics for the month. They'll be with you in prayer as you prepare and preach. They will add to their private prayers at home those names of the sick and troubled you share with them. Christian lay person, how can you creatively support your church (and its outreach) by prayer?

Every local church has the need for basic prayer support. No man can do it alone...there is no such thing as a superman of prayer. Such support is absolutely essential to the spiritual life and growth of any congregation. Without it there is no powerhouse, no power, no light, no life.

While most of this is quite elementary, too many of us are inclined to overlook it. If we do, we do so at the peril of ourselves and our church. A sincere pastor says, "He has called me to do this, His ministry." So acknowledge it as HIS ministry! Seek His guidance and counsel, His grace and power.

In response to the prayers of His people, God the Holy Spirit can create a spiritual climate in which the conversion of individuals becomes a common occurrence. Do you dare to share?

ABOUT THE AUTHOR

Mr. Patterson, an Anglican minister since 1956, has an extensive background in both the ministry and the business world. Prior to entering the ministry he served in the broadcasting industry in both Canada and the United States. This was followed by four years as a salesman and manager in the retail sales field.

Following his ordination, Mr. Patterson served for twelve years in the Diocese of Toronto: four years in a three-point rural parish, followed by a further eight years in a suburban congregation in Metropolitan Toronto. He responded to God's call to a full-time itinerant ministry of evangelism in 1966.

As an itinerant evangelist whose ministry has the endorsement of the General Synod of the Anglican Church of Canada, Mr. Patterson has conducted interdenominational crusades from coast to coast in

Canada and in the United States and the West Indies. On four occasions he has ministered to the Eskimo people in the Canadian Arctic. His overseas ministry includes Japan, the Philippine Islands, India, South Africa, Malawi and Malaysia.

In October, 1966, Mr. Patterson was one of the Canadian delegates to the World Congress on Evangelism in Berlin, Germany. In 1969 he attended the American Congress on Evangelism as a delegate, and in the 1970 Canadian Congress on Evangelism he served as Executive Secretary. More recently, he was an official delegate to the Congress on World Evangelization held in Lausanne, Switzerland, July 1974. Mr. Patterson has also lectured in evangelism at Wycliffe Theological College in Toronto, Canada and at the Protestant Episcopal Seminary, Alexandria, Virginia, U.S.A.

Married in 1949, he has two sons and two daughters.

Those wishing to take advantage of Mr. Patterson's ministry of evangelism may contact him at Invitation to Live Crusades, 7716 Yonge Street, Thornhill, Ontario, Canada, L4J 1W2.

Other books by Rev. Marney Patterson

WHO'S THAT KNOCKING ON MY DOOR
*The Neglected Dimension of Christian
witness*

HIS DOINGS, ON EVERY CONTINENT AND ISLAND
*An intriguing story of God's work for
20 years with Invitation to Live Ministries*

ALIVE & FREE
*An exciting documentary on evangelism
in our time*

WHEN THE SUN REFUSED TO SHINE
*Meditation on the seven last words
from the cross*

NOTES